e v e r y d a y

Low Carb

Cookery

Low Carbohydrate
Recipes for the New Millenium

The Book of Recipes for Whatever Flavor of Low
Carbohydrate Eating Regimen you are Enjoying

by

Alex Haas

Everyday Low Carb Cookery
Low Carbohydrate Recipes for the New Millenium

by

Alex Haas

ISBN 0-9657548-1-2

Table of Contents

Dedication

This is a slightly modified version of my *Everyday Low Carb Cookery*, and it is dedicated, first and foremost, to my family, all of whom need it as badly as I do.

The book is also dedicated to the members of the low carb support group found formerly at lowcarb-list@eskimo.com. Without the support of that group, I would not have been as successful in my weight loss as I have been, and I would not have had the impetus and support to start and continue work on this book. The group was composed of folks from all over the world, in all walks of life who have adopted a low carb eating regimen. This includes all flavors of low carb dieting: Atkins, CAD, *Protein Power*, the body builders and others. They shared their personal experiences and information freely, providing a calming forum for all low carb newcomers. I encourage anyone interested in the low carb lifestyle to subscribe to a similar list and actively participate in the sharing of information.

The book is also dedicated to all those others who are, or who should be, or who want to be on a low carb diet. Hopefully, it will make your commitment to a lifetime of low carb eating all that much easier.

Forward

There are six main issues presently for low carbohydrate eaters. They are: 1) flavor, 2) no sugar, 3) minimize carb grams, 4) fiber, 5) nitrates and nitrites, and 6) aspartame (about which I can say nothing in this book). All recipes are designed to minimize carbs. The other issues are dealt with individually below.

This section gives kind of a "philosophy" of cooking used in these recipes and the recipe selection. You should realize that the recipes are not exhaustive. Quite frankly, there aren't all that many dessert recipes out there for a reason; it's hard to come up with dessert recipes. I've tried to include a few recipes for types of foods that were specifically requested, i.e., tofu and lamb. I've tried to include recipes that will give you a wider variety of foods in your everyday eating, i.e., different ways to cook the types of foods that you normally eat. There are very few "exotic" ingredients. I've tried to include recipes for which there is a minimum amount of labor because a lot of folks don't have all that much time for food preparation. This means, for instance, that I generally don't ask you to peel and mash garlic; you use garlic powder instead. Finally, I've tried to include recipes that will give you the capability to make more "normal" foods. For instance you won't be limited to Bleu Cheese dressing anymore; you can now have low carb Thousand Island Dressing (p. 19).

Food Metaphors - You will notice a few food themes as you are reading through this book. In order to provide variation, I've borrowed foods from other cultures, foods which we don't normally eat on an everyday basis in the U.S. There was no attempt to be exhaustive in this borrowing, I didn't go out and try to get one recipe from every known type of food in the world because I don't know every known food type in the world. However, I have included many recipes of the following types: Cajun, Mexican, German, Russian, Korean, Thai and a few Hungarian and Polish.

Flavor - These recipes are designed to put as much flavor in food as is possible. After all, just because we are dieting, that is not a reason for our food to taste bad. Foods that we are consuming in our low carb eating should taste good so that it is easier to stay with the eating plan. This makes the entire experience pleasant. Keep in mind that humans can taste three things: sweet, sour and hot. These recipes are designed to emphasize these flavors alone and in combination.

Cooking Protein - Protein should be cooked slowly over lower temperatures. Slow cooking causes protein to be tender when it is done. What is the proof of this statement? What happens to milk or eggs when you try to cook them over high heat, say 500 degrees? They become tough. On the other hand, what happens when we boil meat for a long time (at 212 degrees). It is tender. This is what crock-pot cookery was all about - long, slow cooking. This holds for baking and frying as well as the Bar-B-Q and smoking.

It might appear that there is a preponderance of "boiled meat" in these recipes. This is done to tenderize the meat and to ensure that there is a significant amount of stock available for the "sauces". These stocks contain the meat flavor which, when combined with vegetable flavor, are the essence of good cooking. If you don't have stock available, use water with a bouillon cube, although there is about 1 gram of carbs in a bouillon cube, or use commercially prepared canned stock, some of which have no carbohydrates.

One final note about meat cookery. All fowl must be cooked well done because of *salmonella* contamination. Also, there have been recent reports in the media about the effects of eating undercooked (non-fowl) meats and how folks get sick from doing it. I recommend that all non-fowl meats be cooked to at least the "medium" level. The organism (*e. coli*) which was making folks sick is a surface organism. The problem comes about because any ground meat is virtually all surface, so any meat that is ground, such as hamburger or sausages, must also be cooked well done. There are no recipes for "raw" fish in here. All of those diseases which were endemic in Japan from eating uncooked fish became endemic in California with the rise of sushi bars there. All fish must be cooked to well done.

Salt - Salt is included in all of the recipes. Salt enables you to taste the food better. There are complaints among low carb dieters that they are tired of eggs for breakfast. Eggs acquire much more flavor with the addition of salt. If you have high blood pressure, you should consult your physician before adding more salt to your diet. However, we all know that a low carb diet is diuretic in and of itself and there have been several folks whose physicians recommended that they add salt to their diet. For those who worry about the potassium/sodium balance, try the addition of the salt substitute.

Fiber - Those on low carb diets have special needs because they sometimes do not get enough fiber in their diets. Extra fiber can be added into these recipes in the form of wheat bran and psyllium where it would not affect the flavor or texture of the food too much. If psyllium is used, it is unflavored and unsweetened. In many recipes, for instance, sausages or meatballs, psyllium can be used as a binder.

Oil and Acid - The western diet, and especially those on low carb diets, use the combination of oil and acid in a lot of foods. We use oil and vinegar on our salads, we use mayonnaise and its various offshoots, and we use Hollandaise and Hollandaise-like sauces. For oils, we use animal fats and various vegetable oils. For acids we use vinegar, and lemon and lime juices.

Vinegar and Pickling - Several of the recipes in here formally involve pickling, and others, such as making salads, informally involve the pickling process. Pickling is the use of acid and/or salt (and to some extent refrigeration) over time to preserve whatever it is that we are pickling/preserving. The length of time is a function of the surface area. Diced onions and cucumbers pickle in about a day. A beef brisket "corns" in about 3 weeks. Dried sausages, such as Genoa salami, stay in the drying room upwards of 60 days. (A low carb favorite, pepperoni, takes about 3 weeks in the drying room.) The recipes in this book include pickled items which our culture normally does not eat, such as pickled onions, and this gives your diet more variation. Keep in mind that vinegar pickled items, as a rule, do not freeze well, but they shouldn't need to be frozen because they are already preserved.

Sugar - Needless to say, there are no recipes in here which contain sugar. Sugar is poison and one of the primary reasons that we are on this diet in the first place. However, there are recipes which are sweetened, so there must be some kind of standard nomenclature to designate how much of which product you should use, whether it be stevia, saccharin, or, for those outside the U.S., cyclamates, which are presently not FDA approved. In order to be consistent so that everyone can prepare these recipes, we will use the designation "sugar equivalent". So, for instance, when you see, "1 T. sugar equivalent sweetener" you will know that this means to take however much of the sweetener you are using which will be as sweet as 1 tablespoon of sugar. All recipes in this book which require sweetener were tested with saccharin. **Please remember that the use of aspartame in cooking is not recommended because it tends to break down with heat.**

Garlic - This is not a celebration of garlic although garlic is included everywhere it can be. There is only one place in the book where the word "optional" appears in conjunction with the word "garlic". Jeff Smith, "The Frugal Gourmet", once said something to the effect of, "If you have a mate who doesn't like garlic, get a new mate." This is purely understandable from my perspective. However, realizing that there are some folks who are not as enamored with garlic, I decided that moderation should prevail.

Sauces - Sauces and stocks are the essence of good cookery. Sauces and stocks hold much of the flavor and should be eaten. The problem is that low carb foods do not permit thickening of sauces in the traditional manner using flour or cornstarch. Therefore it may be necessary to put a lot of your food in bowls. This suggests soups, and this is the best way to enjoy the flavor of the sauces. Of course, you might have to use a spoon.

Snacks/Gnoshes - One thing that you can do for snacks is to make a double recipe of whatever you are cooking and put it in the refrigerator or freezer. These can be microwaved as needed. The best thing about this is that you know what the carbohydrate count is because you made it. You don't have to worry about the labels being accurate.

Spices - In these recipes, none of the spices were considered to have any carb grams unless they were used in teaspoon quantities. You are permitted to adjust the total carb values and the number of carb grams per serving according to your own whim.

Vegetables - When you are cutting your vegetables, ensure that you always use a stainless steel knife. There are several recipes in this book in which most of the water is cooked out of the vegetables. This process is not unknown to those of you who make spaghetti sauce from scratch or who grew up in the South, which has traditionally suffered the image of "overcooking" vegetables. Water dilutes the flavor.

When to do your cooking - You will find that you do most of your cooking on the weekends. Because you have decided to eat low carb, you are going to become both the food manufacturer and food packager. Remember that you just can't go to the grocery and pick up low carb basic foods like everyone can go to the grocery and pick up low fat foods. You have to make them yourselves. Some of these recipes, such as Bar-B-Q ribs, take a couple of hours of cooking time. However, this is kind of like making bread or pickling.

It takes several hours for you to make bread, but it actually takes only about 20 minutes of your time. From the time you begin to make, for instance, pickled garlic, until the time you eat some is perhaps three weeks, but it takes only about 20 minutes of your actual time. You will also be preparing those things which you want to snack on or have for main dishes that week. Most of the things in here will freeze well so they will not go bad. When you are ready to eat them, just remove them from the freezer and microwave. If you have a microwave at your office, you can just pack your lunch in microwavable dishes and freeze. When you are ready to have this particular dish for lunch, just pull it out of the freezer. The "pickled" salads/slaws will keep well at room temperature several hours, and in a lot of cases, leaving them at room temperature is desirable in order to let the flavors marry. Remember that you cannot do this with mayonnaise-based dressings.

Basics - I would suggest that you make some Pickled Onions (p. 216) and Ketchup (p. 219) immediately as these are used in many other recipes. If you are fond of Thousand Island Dressing (p. 19), then you will need to make Chili Sauce (p. 220) and Sweet Pickle Relish (p. 217) which takes a couple of days to "make".

Nomenclature - The following are the designations used throughout this book:

1 t.	=	1 teaspoon		
1 T.	=	1 tablespoon	=	3 t. by volume
1 c.	=	1 cup	=	16 T. by volume
2 c	=	1 pint		
2 pints	=	1 quart		

Measurements/Quantities - The reader should note that the quantities in the recipes are only suggestions and should, for the most part, be considered to read "More or Less". If you think a recipe needs more garlic (you are blessed) then write it in the margin for the next time you make it. The same goes for salt, vinegar or any other ingredient in a recipe, with a couple of exceptions. In any of the pickling recipes, the salt and vinegar should be considered to be minimum amounts. If you want to add more, that's fine, but do not add less. Do not forget to account for the added or subtracted carbs.

Stocks - Stocks are the essence of good cookery. They are the combinations of meat flavors and vegetable flavors, but because this cookbook is dedicated to every day cooking, I do not give instructions on making stocks. Fortunately, this is one of the foods you can buy off the shelf so you can spend your cooking time preparing other low carb basics. In making soups, I try to include all of the ingredients for making the stocks so that the proper flavors are included. In other recipes there are two substitutes which are readily available to provide this combination of flavors, canned stock and bouillon cubes. These are not as good at the real thing, but they are quicker and easier. Try to find canned stocks and bouillon cubes that don't have any carbs.

Sausages - There are many recipes for sausages in this book. Making sausages is just as easy as or easier than making meatloaf. None of the recipes require the use of sausage casings. When you want to make the sausages, just make them into thin patties as you would a hamburger. The sausage should marinate in the refrigerator overnight. Remember that the sausages must always be cooked well done. When cooking sausages, you may find that you need to add some oil because of any added psyllium or wheat bran. Some sausage recipes are for 5 lb. of meat. This is because it is just as easy to make 5 lb. as it is to make 2 lb., and then you can freeze the extra for later use.

Carb Counts - The calculated carb grams per recipe are not 100% accurate. Some are overestimated slightly and some are underestimated slightly. This is due to several factors. Some companies have more carbs in their products than others. For a couple of items, capers for instance, I was not able to find the carb values in the USDA database and I had to make a "guesstimate". I tended to count spices as 1 gram per teaspoon except for things like dried dill, which don't weigh much more than one gram per teaspoon. Given all this, I will say that the calculated values for individual servings are very close.

Nitrates and Nitrites - There are minimally two recipes in this book which call for curing salt. The curing salt contains the nitrates and nitrites that are used to prevent botulism problems. Botulism is an anaerobic bacterium that cannot grow in a refrigerator. Both of the recipes call for refrigerating the meat while it is curing. I **DO NOT** recommend making these recipes without the curing salt. I have made them with regular table salt, but I do not recommend it. The original Salami and Mortadella recipes called for curing salt, but these sit in the refrigerator only 24-48 hours so the curing salt is used only to maintain the red coloring and is, therefore, unnecessary.

Soup Recipes

French Onion Soup

quantity	ingredient	carb grams
1/2 c.	dry red wine	1
1 T.	Worcestershire Sauce (p. 222)	
1 1/2 lb.	onions, sliced	60
1/4 c.	olive oil	
	enough canned stock to make 3 quarts	
	Total Carbohydrate Grams	61
	Carbohydrate Grams per serving	10.2

Method of Preparation:

The first step is to caramelize the onions. Over medium heat, fry the 1 1/2 lb. of onions in olive oil and salt along with 1/8 cup of water. This should be covered for the first five minutes, just enough time to give the onions a chance to wilt. Remove the lid and continue stirring every 10 minutes. Eventually the water will be evaporated and the onions will start browning. When the onions begin to stick, begin reducing the heat slowly. Ultimately, the onions will become very dark and sticky to the touch. They will almost taste burned. At this point, add the wine, Worcestershire sauce and the stock (half beef and half chicken), cover, bring to a boil, reduce heat and let simmer for 45 minutes, stirring every ten minutes. Serve with Parmesan cheese.

Makes about 3 quarts.

Vegetable Soup
Lenivye Shchi or "Lazy Shchi"
(Russian Cabbage Soup)

Literally translated, this means, "Poor man's soup made the lazy way". I learned to make this soup from my father and have eaten it for the last 25 years (probably three gallons per year with potatoes added). This is a staple in my low carb eating and I try to eat it and a salad (with Vinaigrette Dressing - p. 13) every other evening for supper.

quantity	ingredient	carb grams
1 lb.	good hamburger	
1/3 lb.	cabbage, shredded	3
1	medium carrot, diced	7
3	stalks celery, diced	5
1	medium onion, diced	16
1	can (16 oz.) stewed tomatoes, diced	32
1 T.	dried parsley	
1 T.	garlic powder	6
4 t.	salt	
1 t.	black pepper	
1/2 t.	cayenne pepper (very optional)	
1/2 c.	dry red wine (optional)	1
2 t.	sugar equivalent sweetener	
	enough water to make 3 quarts	
	Total Carbohydrate Grams	70
	Carbohydrate Grams per serving of 1 pint	11.7

Method of Preparation:

Brown the hamburger in your soup pot. Add all of the remaining ingredients except the sweetener. Cover, bring to a boil, reduce heat and let simmer 20 minutes, stirring occasionally (the alcohol in the wine will cook off if you decide to add it). Remove from heat. Add the sweetener and stir. Let sit covered an additional 5 minutes. Stir well before serving. This freezes very well.

Makes about 3 quarts.

Borscht

quantity	ingredient	carb grams
2 lb.	stew beef	
2 T.	olive oil	
1/2 lb.	cabbage, shredded	10
1	medium carrot, diced	7
3	stalks celery, diced	5
1	medium onion, diced	16
1	can (15 oz.) of beets, sliced	32
1 T.	dried parsley	
1 T.	garlic powder	6
2 T.	dill weed	
4 t.	salt	
1 t.	black pepper	
1/2 t.	cayenne pepper (very optional)	
1/2 c.	dry red wine (optional)	1
2 t.	sugar equivalent sweetener	
	enough water to make 3 quarts	
6 dollops	sour cream for serving	3
	Total Carbohydrate Grams	80
	Carbohydrate Grams per serving of 1 pint	13.3

Method of Preparation:

Brown the beef in the oil in your soup pot over medium high heat. Add the cabbage and cook until the cabbage begins to wilt. Add half of the dill weed and all of the remaining ingredients except the beets, the sour cream, and the sweetener. Cover, bring to a boil, reduce heat and let simmer 1 hour, stirring occasionally (the alcohol in the wine will cook off if you decide to add it). Add all of the remaining ingredients except the sour cream and bring to a boil. Remove from heat. Let sit, covered, an additional 5 minutes. Stir well before serving. Serve with a dollop of sour cream on top.

Makes about 3 quarts. This freezes very well.

Fish Chowder

quantity	ingredient	carb grams
1	medium carrot, diced	7
4 oz.	cauliflower, diced	4
1/2	medium yellow onion, diced	8
1/4 c.	scallions, diced	2
3 T.	butter	
1 t.	salt	
1/4 t.	black pepper	
2 t.	dried parsley	
1/4 t.	rosemary	
1/4 t.	thyme	
2 c.	Fish, cut in 1 inch cubes	
1	8 oz.bottle clam juice	
1/2 c.	dry white wine	1
1 c.	half and half	8
	Total Carbohydrate Grams	30
	Carbohydrate Grams per serving	7.5

Method of Preparation:

In a skillet over medium high heat, cook the yellow onion, carrot and cauliflower until the onion begins to turn clear. In this order, add the clam juice, the wine, the half and half and the seasonings. Cover, bring to a boil, reduce heat and simmer 10 minutes. Add the remaining ingredients, bring to a boil, reduce heat and let simmer 5 minutes. Remove from heat and let sit 10 minutes before serving.

Makes 4 servings.

New England Clam Chowder
suggested by Elizabeth Jackson

quantity	ingredient	carb grams
6	slices bacon, diced	
1/2 c.	chopped onion	8
8 oz.	cauliflower, cut into pieces	8
1	can (3 1/2 oz) minced clams	
2 c.	water	
1/2 c.	heavy cream	3
1 t.	salt	
1/2 t.	black pepper	
1/2 t.	dill weed	
	Total Carbohydrate Grams	19
	Carbohydrate Grams per serving	4.8

Method of Preparation:

In sauce pan over medium heat, fry bacon until crisp. Remove crisp bacon from fat and set aside. To the bacon fat add the onion, cauliflower, water, juice from canned clams and the seasoning. Cook at a slow boil until cauliflower is soft (10-15 min.). Add clams and remove from heat. Let sit for 5 minutes, then add cream and bacon.

Makes 4 servings.

Hint – 1 cup is equivalent to 16 tablespoons.

Manhattan Clam Chowder

quantity	ingredient	carb grams
4	slices bacon, diced	
1/4	medium onion, diced	4
2 t.	garlic powder	4
1 T.	dried parsley	
1/2	medium carrot, diced	4
2	stalks celery, diced	3
8 oz.	stewed tomatoes, diced	16
2	cans (3 1/2 oz.) diced clams	
1 t.	salt	
1/4 t.	black pepper	
1 t.	thyme	
1	bay leaf	
	Total Carbohydrate Grams	31
	Carbohydrate Grams per serving	15.5

Method of Preparation:

Fry the onion over medium heat until well browned. Increase heat to medium high and fry the carrots and celery for about 2 minutes. Add the onions and cook until they become clear. Drain the clams reserving the juice. Add everything to the soup pot except the clams. Cover and bring to a boil to a boil. Reduce heat and let simmer 30 minutes. Stir in the clams and let sit 5 minutes before serving.

Makes 2 servings.

Bouillabaisse

quantity	ingredient	carb grams
1 c.	water	
1 c.	clam juice	
1	can (16 oz.) stewed tomatoes, diced	32
2 t.	Worcestershire Sauce (p. 222)	
3	bouillon cubes	3
1/2	medium yellow onion, diced	8
1/4 c.	scallions, diced	2
1 t.	garlic powder	2
1 T.	dried basil	
1 t.	dried dillweed	
2 T.	olive oil	
1/2 lb.	fish (see directions)	
1 lb.	mussels	
1/2 lb.	shrimp	
1	can (11 oz.) lobster meat thawed	
	Total Carbohydrate Grams	47
	Carbohydrate Grams per serving	11.5

Method of Preparation:

For fish you can use any of the following: cod, haddock, or halibut. In your large pan, cook the yellow onion in the oil over medium heat until it begins to become clear. Add the scallions and cook an additional 2 minutes. Add the liquids, the spices, and the bouillon cubes, bring to a boil, cover and simmer 10 minutes. Add the fish and the mussels, and cook until the fish turns opaque and the mussels open, about 5 minutes. Add the shrimp and lobster and bring to a boil. Turn off heat and let sit five minutes before serving. If the shrimp are raw, they should be added along with the fish and the mussels.

Makes 4 servings.

Simple Tomato Fish Soup

quantity	ingredient	carb grams
1	medium onion, diced	16
2 t.	garlic powder	4
2 T.	olive oil	
1	can (16 oz.) stewed tomatoes, diced	32
1	bottle clam juice	
2 T.	lemon juice	2
2 T.	dried parsley	
1 t.	oregano	1
1/2 c.	dry red wine	1
2 lb.	white fish fillets, cut bite-sized	
1 t.	salt	
1/2 t.	pepper	
	Total Carbohydrate Grams	46
	Carbohydrate Grams per serving	11.5

Method of Preparation:

Sauté the onions in the oil over medium heat until the onions are clear. Add the liquids and the spices and simmer, covered, 10 minutes. Add the remaining ingredients and simmer 5 minutes. Remove from heat and let sit 10 minutes before serving.

Makes 4 servings.

Hearty Fish and Tomato Soup

quantity	ingredient	carb grams
2 lb.	fish fillets, cut into 1 inch cubes	
6 T.	butter	
4 oz.	onion, diced	8
4 oz.	celery, diced	3
4 oz.	bell pepper, diced	3
4 oz.	carrot, diced	6
1	8 oz. bottle clam juice	
1	can (16 oz.) stewed tomatoes, diced	32
2 c.	tomato juice	32
2 T.	pickling spice	
2 t.	garlic powder	4
1 1/2 t.	salt	
1 t.	paprika	1
1 T.	Worcestershire Sauce (p. 222)	
1/4 t.	Tabasco sauce	
	Total Carbohydrate Grams	89
	Carbohydrate Grams per serving	14.8

Method of Preparation:

Tie the pickling spice in a bag made of cheesecloth. If you don't have cheesecloth, put the pickling spice in the clam juice, cover and simmer for one hour and then strain out the solids. You do NOT want the pickling spice to remain in your soup; you just want the flavor. Melt the butter in your pan over medium high heat. Sauté the onions, celery, green peppers and carrots about 5 minutes or until the onions begin to clear. Add the liquids, the spice bag and the remaining seasonings and simmer, covered, for 30 minutes (if you are not using the spice bag, this can be reduced to 15 minutes). Add the fish, bring to a boil and simmer for 5 minutes. Remove from heat and let sit 5 minutes before serving. Remove the spice bag before serving.

Makes 6 servings.

Seafood Okra Gumbo

quantity	ingredient	carb grams
1 lb.	okra, cut in 1/2 inch pieces	34
3 T.	olive oil	
1	medium onion, diced	16
1	medium bell pepper, diced	6
2	stalks celery, diced	3
2 lb.	Shrimp, cooked	
1 lb.	uncooked crab meat	
1 T.	garlic powder	6
2 T.	dried parsley	
1	8 oz. bottle clam juice	
1	can (15 oz) stewed tomatoes, diced	30
2	bay leaves	
2 T.	Worcestershire Sauce (p. 222)	
2 t.	salt	
1 t.	black pepper	
1 t.	cayenne pepper	1
	Total Carbohydrate Grams	96
	Carbohydrate Grams per serving	16.0

Method of Preparation:

In your soup pot, sauté the okra over medium to low heat until it is wilted and real soft to touch, about 30 minutes. Add the onions, celery, bell pepper and carrot and cook until the onions begin to turn clear. Add liquids and seasoning, cover, bring to a boil, and simmer 30 minutes. Remove the bay leaves. Add the remaining ingredients, remove from the heat and let sit 10 minutes before serving.

Makes 6 servings.

Chicken-Smoked Sausage Gumbo

quantity	ingredient	carb grams
1 lb.	okra, cut in 1/2 inch pieces	34
2 qt.	water	
3 T.	olive oil	
1	medium onion, diced	16
1	medium bell pepper, diced	6
2	stalks celery, diced	3
3 lb.	chicken, uncooked	
1 lb.	smoked polish sausage, sliced	16
1 T.	garlic powder	6
2 T.	dried parsley	
1	can (15 oz) stewed tomatoes, diced	30
2	bay leaves	
1 t.	thyme	
1 t.	basil	
1 T.	salt	
1 t.	black pepper	
1 t.	cayenne pepper	1
	Total Carbohydrate Grams	112
	Carbohydrate Grams per serving	18.7

Cut your chicken into 8 pieces. Cover with water, cover the pan, bring to a boil and simmer for about an hour until the chicken is tender. Set the stock aside for later use. Allow the chicken to cool, remove from the bone and set aside. Meanwhile in your soup pot, sauté the okra over medium to low heat until it is wilted and real soft to touch, about 30 minutes. Add the onions, celery, bell pepper and carrot, and cook until the onions begin to turn clear. Add liquids, including the chicken stock and seasoning. Cover, bring to a boil, and simmer 30 minutes. Remove the bay leaves. Add the remaining ingredients and let simmer an additional 10 minutes. Remove from the heat and let sit 10 minutes before serving.

Makes 6 servings.

German Gulaschsuppe
(Goulash Soup)

quantity	ingredient	carb grams
1 c.	onion, sliced	16
4 T.	olive oil	
3	medium green peppers, sliced	18
3 T.	tomato paste	8
2 lb.	stew beef	
1/2 t.	cayenne pepper	
2 t.	garlic powder	4
6 c.	canned beef broth	6
1 T.	lemon juice	1
1/2 t.	caraway seeds	
	Total Carbohydrate Grams	53
	Carbohydrate Grams per serving	8.8

Method of Preparation:

In 2 T. of oil fry the meat over medium heat until it is well browned. Remove the meat from the pan, reserving as much oil as possible. Add the remaining oil to the skillet. Fry the onions until they are clear. Add the green peppers, cover and cook about 10 minutes. Add all other ingredients, cover, bring to a boil and simmer 1 1/2 hours, stirring every 20 minutes.

Makes 6 servings.

Salad Recipes

Vinaigrette

This is a staple of my own diet. This makes a salad that is better than you can get at the Olive Garden. The carbs are negligible.

quantity	ingredient	carb grams
1 c.	olive oil	
1/2 c.	vinegar (any type except white)	
1/2 c.	water	
2 t.	celery salt	1
1/2 t.	pepper	
1/2 t.	dried mustard	
1 t.	Italian seasoning	1
2 t.	garlic powder	4
1 t.	onion powder	1
2 t.	sugar equivalent sweetener	
	Total Carbohydrate Grams	6
	Carbohydrate Grams per serving of 1 T.	0.2

Method of Preparation:

Put all ingredients except the oil in a jar and shake. Let sit for about 15 minutes. Shake again and add the oil. Keep refrigerated. Shake very well before serving. Actually, using a small dipper facilitates serving.

There are several variations on this. My particular favorite is to add 1/4 c. of Parmesan cheese and mix with the dry ingredients. For those who like bleu cheese dressing, mix the vinegar and dry ingredients in a bowl. Before mixing in the oil, mix the bleu cheese with the vinegar. For those who like creamy dressing, use mayonnaise (with perhaps some sour cream) instead of olive oil.

Makes about 2 cups.

Southwestern Vinaigrette

quantity	ingredient	carb grams
1 c.	olive oil	
1/2 c.	Faux Balsamic Vinegar (p. 223)	
1/2 c.	water	
1 t.	salt	
2	green chili peppers, diced	2
1/4 c.	Dijon mustard	
1 t.	Italian seasoning	1
2 t.	garlic powder	4
1 t.	onion powder	1
	Total Carbohydrate Grams	8
	Carbohydrate Grams per serving of 1 T.	0.3

Method of Preparation:

Add the peppers to the vinegar in the mixing bowl and let sit 15 minutes. Add the water and the dry ingredients, mix well and let sit another 15 minutes. Add the mustard and mix well. Add the oil, mix well, pour in your storage jar and refrigerate. Mix well before serving.

Makes about 2 ½ cups.

Hint – Cheeses tend to be calorie dense and they all contain at least a half gram of carbs per ounce.

Caesar Salad Dressing

This dressing is made with mayonnaise instead of raw eggs for safety purposes.

quantity	ingredient	carb grams
1 ¼ c.	mayonnaise	
2 T.	lemon juice	2
1 t.	sugar equivalent sweetener	
2 t.	garlic powder	4
1 t.	onion powder	1
1 t.	dry mustard	1
½ t.	black pepper	
½ oz.	anchovy fillets mashed with the oil	
½ c.	grated Parmesan cheese	3
	Total Carbohydrate Grams	11
	Carbohydrate Grams per serving of 1 T.	0.5

Method of Preparation:

Dissolve the sweetener in the lemon juice. Add the spices, and let sit about 15 minutes. Add the remaining ingredients, stir well, place in a jar and let sit refrigerated, overnight if possible.

Makes about 1 1/2 cups.

Ranch-Style Dressing

quantity	ingredient	carb grams
1 c.	mayonnaise	
1 c.	buttermilk	13
1/4 c.	Pickled Onions (p. 216)	4
1 T.	dried chives	
2 t.	garlic powder	4
1 T.	dried parsley	
1/2 t.	paprika	
1/4 t.	cayenne pepper	
1 t.	celery salt	
1/2 t.	black pepper	
	Total Carbohydrate Grams	21
	Carbohydrate Grams per serving of 1 T.	0.5

Method of Preparation:

Mix all ingredients. Refrigerate overnight if possible.

Makes about 2 1/2 cups

Bleu Cheese Dressing

quantity	ingredient	carb grams
1 c.	mayonnaise	
1/4 c.	Pickled Onions (p. 216)	4
2 t.	garlic powder	4
2 T.	dried parsley	
1/2 c.	sour cream	3
2 T.	lemon juice	4
2 t.	sugar equivalent sweetener	
1/4 c.	crumbled bleu cheese	1
1 t.	celery salt	
1/2 t.	red pepper sauce	
	Total Carbohydrate Grams	16
	Carbohydrate Grams per serving of 1 T.	0.7

Method of Preparation:

Mix everything in a bowl. Place in a jar. Let sit in the refrigerator overnight if possible.

Makes about 2 1/2 cups.

Garlic-Bleu Cheese Salad

suggested by Crystal Feist

This is one of the few recipes in which it is suggested that you use fresh garlic.

quantity	ingredient	carb grams
3 T.	olive oil	
1 T.	Faux Balsamic Vinegar (p. 223)	
1/2 t.	salt	
2	cloves garlic, diced finely	2
1/2 t.	onion powder	
1/2 c.	bleu cheese (at room temperature), crumbled	4
1/4	head lettuce, torn for a salad	2
	Total Carbohydrate Grams	8
	Carbohydrate Grams per serving	8

Method of Preparation:

In your salad bowl, using a fork, mash the garlic with the salt until the garlic is almost a paste. Add the oil and mix thoroughly. Add the vinegar and onion powder and mix. Mix in the bleu cheese with the fork again making a paste. Pour over the lettuce and toss.

Makes one serving.

Hint – One ounce of water is equivalent to two tablespoons.

Thousand Island Dressing

quantity	ingredient	carb grams
1 c.	mayonnaise	
2 T.	Chili Sauce (p. 220)	2
1 T.	dried parsley	
1	medium bell pepper, diced	6
1/2 t.	salt	
1 T.	paprika	3
1 t.	garlic powder	2
1/4 t.	cayenne pepper (optional)	
1/4 c.	Pickled Onions (p. 216)	4
1/4 c.	Pickled Onion juice (optional)	
1/4 c.	Sweet Pickle Relish (p. 217)	3
	Total Carbohydrate Grams	20
	Carbohydrate Grams per serving of 1 T.	0.6

Method of Preparation:

In a saucepan, bring the Pickled Onion juice to a boil; add the bell pepper, stir, and cover. Bring to a boil again, remove from heat, and let cool. Mix all ingredients in a bowl, put in a jar, and refrigerate. Can dilute further if desired with the Pickled Onion juice.

Makes about 2 cups.

Hint – Watch for hidden carbs in the little pink and blue sweetener packets.

French Salad Dressing (1)

quantity	ingredient	carb grams
1/2 c.	Pickled Onions (p. 216)	8
1 c.	olive oil	
1/2 c.	Chile Sauce	6
1/2 c.	sugar equivalent sweetener	
1 c.	vinegar	
1/2 c.	water	
1/2 t.	salt	
1/2 t.	black pepper	
1/2 t.	dry mustard	
1 t.	garlic powder	2
1 T.	paprika	3
	Total Carbohydrate Grams	19
	Carbohydrate Grams per serving of 1 T.	0.5

Method of Preparation:

Mix all ingredients thoroughly. Should keep in a jar in the refrigerator several weeks.

Makes about 3 1/2 cups.

French Salad Dressing (2)

quantity	ingredient	carb grams
1/2 c.	Pickled Onions (p. 216)	8
3 c.	olive oil	
1 c.	sugar equivalent sweetener	
1 c.	vinegar	
1/2 t.	celery salt	
1 t.	black pepper	
4 t.	dry mustard	4
1 t.	garlic powder	2
4 t.	paprika	4
	Total Carbohydrate Grams	18
	Carbohydrate Grams per serving of 1 T.	0.5

Method of Preparation:

Mix all ingredients. Should keep in a jar in the refrigerator several weeks.

Makes about 4 1/2 cups.

Green Goddess Dressing

quantity	ingredient	carb grams
6	anchovy filets, mashed well	
1/4 c.	finely diced scallions with tops	2
2 T.	dried parsley	
4 T.	dried chives	2
1/4 c.	Pickled Onions (p. 216)	4
1/2 t.	dried tarragon	
2 c.	mayonnaise	
1/4 c.	tarragon vinegar	
2 t.	garlic powder	4
	Total Carbohydrate Grams	12
	Carbohydrate Grams per serving of 1 T	0.3

Method of Preparation:

Mix all ingredients and let sit refrigerated at least two hours.

Makes about 2 1/2 cups.

Hint – Watch out for hidden carbs in the form of alcohol sugars, such as sorbitol and manitol.

Avocado Salad Dressing

quantity	ingredient	carb grams
1 c.	olive oil	
1	avocado	14
1/4 c.	lemon juice	8
1/4 c.	sugar equivalent sweetener	
1 t.	dry mustard	1
1/2 t.	salt	
1 t.	paprika	1
1 t.	garlic powder	2
1/4 c.	Pickled Onions (p. 216)	4
	Total Carbohydrate Grams	30
	Carbohydrate Grams per serving of 1 T.	0.9

Method of Preparation:

Peel the avocado and remove the seed. Place in a bowl with the lemon juice and mash well with a fork. Add remaining ingredients and stir well. Store refrigerated in a covered container.

Makes about 2 cups.

Tofu Dressing

quantity	ingredient	carb grams
1/2 c.	olive oil	
4 oz.	soft tofu, drained	4
3 T.	Dijon mustard	3
4 T.	lemon juice	8
2 t.	garlic powder	4
1/4 t.	salt	
1/4 c.	Pickled Onions (p. 216)	4
1 T.	dried chives	
	Total Carbohydrate Grams	23
	Carbohydrate Grams per serving of 1 T.	1.0

Method of Preparation:

Puree lemon juice and tofu in blender or processor until smooth. Add remaining ingredients and continue processing until everything is smooth. Transfer mixture to a jar. Cover and chill. Will keep up to a week or more.

Makes about 1 1/2 cups.

Three Pepper Salad

quantity	ingredient	carb grams
1	medium red bell pepper, sliced	6
1	medium yellow bell pepper, sliced	6
1	medium green bell pepper, sliced	6
1/4 c.	Pickled Onions (p. 216)	4
2 T.	olive oil	
2 t.	Faux Balsamic Vinegar (p. 223)	
1/2 t.	salt	
1 t.	garlic powder	2
1 t.	oregano	
1 t.	basil	1
	Total Carbohydrate Grams	25
	Carbohydrate Grams per serving	6.0

Method of Preparation:

Place the peppers and salt in a microwavable salad bowl. Microwave for 2 minutes. Stir. Keep up this process until the peppers are too hot to touch and beginning to wilt. Add the remaining ingredients, stir and let sit at room temperature for about 2 hours, stirring every half hour. Can serve immediately or refrigerate. Will keep several days refrigerated.

Makes about 4 servings.

Wilted Lettuce Salad

This salad is especially good in the winter.

quantity	ingredient	carb grams
1/2	head of lettuce, quartered	3
1/2	medium onion, sliced	8
3	slices of bacon, diced	
1 T.	olive oil	
2 T.	Faux Balsamic Vinegar (p. 223)	
1 t.	Italian seasoning	1
1 t.	garlic powder	2
1 T.	water	
.		
	Total Carbohydrate Grams	14
	Carbohydrate Grams per serving	7.0

Method of Preparation:

In a very large pan, fry the bacon in the olive oil over medium to low heat until it is well browned and crispy. Increase the heat to medium high, add the onion and cook it until it is about clear. Add the water, vinegar and spices and bring to a boil. Turn off the heat, add the lettuce, stir and cover. After one minute, stir again and serve immediately. Salt to taste.

Makes 2 servings.

Broccoli Salad with Tarragon Dressing

quantity	ingredient	carb grams
1 lb.	broccoli, trimmed and cut into florets	15
2 t.	garlic powder	4
2 T.	white wine vinegar	
2 T.	Sweet Pickle Relish (p. 217)	1
2 T.	chopped chives	1
2 T.	chopped fresh tarragon	2
1/2 t.	salt	
1/4 t.	pepper	
1/3 c.	olive oil	
	Total Carbohydrate Grams	23
	Carbohydrate Grams per serving	5.8

Method of Preparation:

Blanch the broccoli in boiling water for 1 minute, then cool in ice water. Drain well before putting it in a bowl. Mix the remaining ingredients in a separate bowl and pour over the broccoli. Stir well a couple of time. Let sit refrigerated a couple of hours before serving. Will keep several days.

Makes 4 servings.

Mushroom Salad

quantity	ingredient	carb grams
1 lb.	mushrooms	16
2 t.	garlic powder	4
2 T.	Faux Balsamic Vinegar (p. 223)	
2 T.	Pickled Onions (p. 216)	2
2 T.	chopped chives	
1/2 t.	salt	
1/4 t.	pepper	
1/3 c.	olive oil	
	Total Carbohydrate Grams	22
	Carbohydrate Grams per serving	5.5

Method of Preparation:

Blanch the mushrooms in boiling water for 1 minute, then cool in ice water. Drain well before putting it in a bowl. Mix the remaining ingredients in a separate bowl and pour over the mushrooms. Stir well a couple of time. Let sit refrigerated a couple of hours before serving. Will keep several days.

Makes 4 servings.

German Mushroom Salad

quantity	ingredient	carb grams
1 lb.	fresh mushrooms	16
1/4 c.	Sweet Pickle Relish (p. 217)	3
1/4 c.	Pickled Onions (p. 216)	4
2 t.	garlic powder	4
1	medium tomato seeded and, diced finely	8
1/2 c.	olive oil	
1/4 c.	Faux Balsamic Vinegar (p. 223)	
1 t.	salt	
1 t.	sugar equivalent sweetener	
	Total Carbohydrate Grams	35
	Carbohydrate Grams per serving	7.0

Method of Preparation:

Slice the mushrooms in half. Place the mushrooms, vinegar, sweetener and salt in your salad bowl. Mix well and let sit an hour stirring every 15 minutes. Add the tomato and let sit an additional 30 minutes stirring every 15 minutes. Add all other ingredients. Let sit in the refrigerator several hours before serving if possible.

Makes 5 servings.

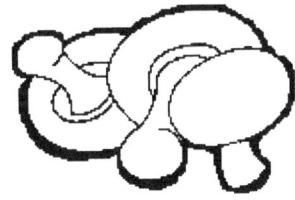

Cucumber-Zucchini (German Style)

quantity	ingredient	carb grams
1/2 lb.	peeled and sliced cucumbers	5
1/2 lb.	sliced zucchini	6
1/2	medium onion, sliced	8
1/4 c.	white vinegar	
2 T.	sugar equivalent sweetener	
1/2 c.	water	
2 t.	salt	
1 t.	garlic powder	2
1/2 t.	black pepper	
1/2 c.	sour cream	3
2 T.	chopped chives, either fresh or dried	1
	Total Carbohydrate Grams	25
	Carbohydrate Grams per serving	6.3

Method of Preparation:

Place zucchini and cucumber in the salad bowl and add 1 teaspoon of salt and stir. Let sit at room temperature about an hour to wilt the vegetables. Pour water off the vegetables and gently squeeze out more liquid. Add remaining ingredients except the sour cream and chives, stir and refrigerate for a couple of hours. About an hour before serving, add the sour cream and stir again. Sprinkle chives over bowl just before serving. This will keep several days.

Makes about 4 servings.

Bar-B-Q Slaw

This type of slaw is traditionally served with Bar-B-Q in northern Alabama and southern Tennessee.

quantity	ingredient	carb grams
1 lb.	cabbage, sliced or shredded	18
1/2	medium onion, diced	8
1/2 c.	water	
1/2 c.	vinegar	
1 1/2 t.	salt	
5 T.	sugar equivalent sweetener	
	Total Carbohydrate Grams	26
	Carbohydrate Grams per serving	6.5

Method of Preparation:

Bring all ingredients except the cabbage to a boil and remove from heat. Add the cabbage, stir and let cool. Stir. Place in a bowl or jar. This should be kept refrigerated and it will keep a couple of weeks. Ready in a couple of hours.

Makes 4 servings.

Hint – For water, a pint is a pound the world around.

Coleslaw

quantity	ingredient	carb grams
1 lb.	cabbage, shredded	18
1/2	medium onion, diced	8
1/2	medium bell pepper, diced	3
2 T.	vinegar	
2 T.	sugar equivalent sweetener	
1 1/2 t.	salt	
1/2 c.	mayonnaise	
1 t.	dry mustard	1
1 t.	garlic powder	2
	Total Carbohydrate Grams	32
	Carbohydrate Grams per serving	5.3

Method of Preparation:

Place the vegetables in your salad bowl and toss. Mix everything else in a small bowl and pour over the vegetables. Toss and let sit at room temperature a couple of hours so that the vegetables begin to wilt, stirring occasionally. Refrigerate. Best if made the day before. Will keep several days in the refrigerator.

Makes about 6 servings.

Eastern Carolina Style Slaw

quantity	ingredient	carb grams
1 1/2 lb.	cabbage, finely shredded	27
1/4 c.	scallions, diced	2
1 c.	mayonnaise	
2 T.	vinegar	
2 t.	celery salt	
2 T.	sugar equivalent sweetener	
	Total Carbohydrate Grams	29
	Carbohydrate Grams per serving	4.8

Method of Preparation:

Mix the cabbage and onion in a salad bowl. In a separate bowl, combine the mayonnaise, sweetener, vinegar and celery salt. Mix in with the cabbage. Refrigerate until ready to serve. Serve with Eastern Carolina Bar-B-Q (p. 81).

Makes 6 servings.

Korean Slaw

quantity	ingredient	carb grams
1 lb.	cabbage, shredded	18
1/2	medium onion, diced	8
1/2	medium bell pepper, diced	3
4 T.	vinegar	
4 T.	sugar equivalent sweetener	
4 oz.	fresh snow peas, sliced very thinly	7
2 t.	salt	
1/2 c.	light sesame oil	
1 T.	sesame seeds	2
2 t.	garlic powder	4
	red pepper sauce (optional)	
	Total Carbohydrate Grams	42
	Carbohydrate Grams per serving	7.0

Method of Preparation:

Place the vegetables in your salad bowl and toss. Mix everything else except the pepper sauce in a small bowl and pour over the vegetables. Toss and let sit at room temperature several hours so that the vegetables begin to wilt, stirring occasionally. Refrigerate. Best if made the day before. Will keep several days in the refrigerator.

Makes about 6 servings.

Cucumber Salad

quantity	ingredient	carb grams
2 lb.	salad cucumbers peeled and sliced	18
2 T.	olive oil	
1/4 c.	Pickled Onions (p. 216)	4
1 t.	salt	
1/2 t.	salt	
1/4 t.	pepper	
1 t.	garlic powder	2
	Faux Balsamic Vinegar (p. 223) to taste	
	Total Carbohydrate Grams	24
	Carbohydrate Grams per serving	6.0

Method of Preparation:

Place the cucumbers in your salad bowl. Sprinkle over 1 t. salt and mix well. Let sit at room temperature several hours to render the water from the cucumbers. Drain the water off, squeezing the cucumbers slightly. Add the remaining ingredients and mix well. Let sit at room temperature another hour or so. Taste to ensure that you have enough acid. Refrigerate overnight.

Makes about 4 servings.

Korean Cucumber Salad

quantity	ingredient	carb grams
2 c.	water	
4 t.	salt	
4 c.	medium to small cucumbers	12
1/2 c.	scallions, diced	4
1 T.	wine vinegar	
2 t.	garlic powder	4
1 T.	sesame seeds	2
2 T.	light sesame oil	
4 t.	sugar equivalent sweetener	
1/2 t.	cayenne pepper	
	Total Carbohydrate Grams	20
	Carbohydrate Grams per serving	5.0

Method of Preparation:

If the cucumbers were purchased from a grocery store, they must be peeled to remove the wax. Slice the cucumbers about 1/8 inch thick. If the seeds of the cucumbers are tough, they must be removed. Bring the water and salt to a boil. Add the cucumbers and let simmer 1 minute. Remove from heat and let cool. Put in a jar and let sit on the cupboard 24 hours. To prepare the salad, drain the cucumbers and rinse with cold water. Drain. Dice the lower half of each scallion. Add the remaining dry ingredients, the diced onions, and the vinegar to the cucumbers and mix well for a few minutes. Add the oil and mix well. Refrigerate for a day. Serve about 2 ounces per person.

Makes about 4 cups.

Tomato Pepper Salad with Tuna

quantity	ingredient	carb grams
8 oz.	canned artichokes	24
7 oz.	tuna in oil	
2	medium tomatoes seeds removed and, diced	16
1	medium cucumber, sliced	5
1/4 c.	Pickled Onions (p. 216)	4
1	medium green pepper, sliced	6
3 oz.	black olives	3
6	pepperocini (small warm peppers pickled)	5
1/2 c.	Vinaigrette (p. 13)	3
2 t.	Dijon mustard	
1/4 t.	black pepper	
1 t.	salt	
2 t.	sugar equivalent sweetener	
	Total Carbohydrate Grams	66
	Carbohydrate Grams per serving	11.0

Method of Preparation:

Mix the tomatoes, salt, pepper and the sweetener and let sit at room temperature for 15 minutes, stirring every 5 minutes. Cut the artichokes to bite sized. Mix the tomatoes, artichokes, peppers, onions, tuna, olives and pepperocini in a salad bowl. In a small bowl mix the vinaigrette and mustard thoroughly to make the dressing for the salad. Spoon the dressing over the salad ingredients and mix. Wait at least an hour before serving.

Makes 6 servings.

Main Courses - Beef

Corned Beef and Cabbage (1)
(no nitrates or nitrites)

quantity	ingredient	carb grams
5 lb.	stew beef	
3 lb.	cabbage cut in 8ths	54
1	medium onion, sliced	16
1	medium carrot, diced	7
2	stalks celery, diced	3
1 T.	dried parsley	
1 T.	garlic powder	6
2 T.	sugar equivalent sweetener	
4 T.	pickling spice	
2	bay leaves	
2 t.	caraway seeds	3
2 t.	black peppercorns	
1 T.	salt	
3/4 c.	malt vinegar	
1	can (12 oz.) low carb beer	3
	enough water to cover the beef	
	coarse grain and/or Dijon mustard for serving	
	Total Carbohydrate Grams	92
	Carbohydrate Grams per serving	11.5

Corned Beef and Cabbage (1)

Method of Preparation:

This is a 2-stage process. First you are going to "corn" the beef and then at a later date, you will finish the dish. In a large pan, bring the beef, water, beer, vinegar, sweetener, pickling spice, bay leaves, caraway seed, peppercorns and salt to a boil. Let simmer covered an hour and a half stirring every 20 minutes. Turn off the heat and let cool to room temperature. Place in a covered container in the refrigerator for a couple of days. After it has set for a few days you can now freeze it for later use or go on to the next stage keeping in mind that it can be frozen at any point after this. Remove from the refrigerator and remove the meat from the broth. Strain the broth to remove all of the spices and returns the broth to the meat. Add the remaining ingredients to the meat, bring to a boil, and simmer, covered, about and hour.

Makes 8 servings.

Hint – A teaspoon is equivalent to five grams of water.

Corned Beef and Cabbage (2)

This dish is traditionally served with potatoes, but we don't need them.

quantity	ingredient	carb grams
4 lb.	uncooked corned beef	
3 lb.	Cabbage, cut to bite-size	60
1	medium carrot, diced	7
3	stalks celery, diced	5
1	medium onion, diced	16
1 T.	dried parsley	
1 T.	garlic powder	6
1 t.	black pepper	
2 t.	sugar equivalent sweetener	
1 c.	dry white wine	1
	enough water to make 3 quarts	
	Total Carbohydrate Grams	95
	Carbohydrate Grams per serving	13.6

Method of Preparation:

Remove the large layer of fat but don't throw it away (this step isn't entirely necessary). Place the corned beef and the fat in two quarts of water, cover, bring to a boil, reduce the heat and let simmer two hours. Remove the meat and fat from the stock and add everything else to the stock except the sweetener. Again, bring it to a boil, then reduce the heat and simmer. Throw the fat away (there is plenty remaining). When the corned beef cools, cut it into bite-sized pieces and return it to the soup. Simmer for at least one hour. Add the sweetener and simmer an additional 10 minutes.

Makes about 7 servings

Corned Beef

quantity	ingredient	carb grams
2 lb.	stew beef	
1 c.	pickling salt	
1 c.	water	
4 t.	black pepper	
3 T.	ginger	
2 t.	ground clove	
4	bay leaves	
4 T.	sugar equivalent sweetener	
1 t.	nutmeg	
2 t.	paprika	
4 t.	mustard seed	
1 t.	caraway seed	
4 T.	garlic powder	
	Total Carbohydrate Grams	
	Carbohydrate Grams per serving	0

Method of Preparation:

Bring everything except the beef to a boil. Remove from heat and let cool to room temperature. Place the beef in a non-metal container. Pour the liquid over and stir. Keep refrigerated 7 to 10 days, stirring every second day. You must ensure that all of the meat is kept submerged under the brine. This is facilitated by having a container which is taller than it is wide. To prepare, remove the meat from the brine. Cover with cold water and bring to a boil. Throw the water away. Repeat two times. This is the stage that the corned beef is considered ready to be cooked. Cover with cold water again, bring to a boil and simmer covered about an hour and a half. At this stage you can begin to prepare the Corned Beef and Cabbage or Crockpot Corned Beef and Cabbage. Count this as 0 carbs because none of the seasoning is eaten with the meat.

Crockpot Corned Beef and Cabbage

quantity	ingredient	carb grams
1	recipe Corned Beef (p. 41)	
2 c.	stock from Corned Beef	
2 T.	sugar equivalent sweetener	
3 T.	white vinegar	
1	medium onion, sliced	16
2 lb.	cabbage, sliced coarsely	36
1/2 t.	black pepper	
2	whole bay leaves	
2 t.	garlic powder	4
1	medium carrot, sliced	7
3	stalks celery, sliced	5
	Total Carbohydrate Grams	68
	Carbohydrate Grams per serving	17.0

Method of Preparation:

Place all ingredients in the crock-pot with the cabbage on top. Cook 5-6 hours on high.

Makes 4 servings.

Bar-B-Q Corned Beef

quantity	ingredient	carb grams
1	recipe cooked Corned Beef (p. 41)	
1/2 c.	Bar-B-Q Sauce (p. 224)	6
2 T.	prepared salad mustard	
	Total Carbohydrate Grams	6
	Carbohydrate Grams per serving	1.5

Method of Preparation:

Place all ingredients in a large pan. Bring to a boil and let simmer uncovered until the sauce thickens.

Makes 4 servings.

Hint – One ounce is equivalent to 28.4 grams of water.

Corned Beef Hash

quantity	ingredient	carb grams
1 lb.	cooked Corned Beef (p. 41), diced finely	
1	egg	1
2 T.	olive oil	
4 oz.	onion, diced finely	8
4 oz.	bell pepper, diced finely	3
1/2 t.	garlic powder	1
1/4 t.	salt	
1/4 t.	dry mustard (optional)	
	Total Carbohydrate Grams	13
	Carbohydrate Grams per serving	6.5

Method of Preparation:

Fry the onions and peppers in 1 T. oil over medium heat until the onions are clear. Remove from heat and let cool to room temperature. In a bowl, mix everything thoroughly together. Separate into 4 patties. Fry in 1 T. of olive oil until browned well on both sides.

Makes 4 servings.

Pastrami

quantity	ingredient	carb grams
2 lb.	stew beef	
1 c.	water	
1 c.	pickling salt	
3 T.	black pepper	
2 T.	garlic powder	
3 T.	sugar equivalent sweetener	
4 T.	pickling spice	
1/2 c.	white vinegar	
1 T.	onion powder	
	Total Carbohydrate Grams	
	Carbohydrate Grams per serving	3.0

Method of Preparation:

Bring everything except the beef to a boil. Remove from heat and let cool to room temperature. Place the beef in a non-metal container. Pour the liquid over and stir. Keep refrigerated 7 to 10 days, stirring every second day. You must ensure that all of the meat is kept submerged under the brine. This is facilitated by having a container which is taller than it is wide.

To prepare, remove the meat from the brine. Cover with cold water and bring to a boil. Throw the water away. Repeat two times. The third time, add 1 small, diced carrot, 2 diced stalks of celery, 1/2 diced medium onion, 2 T. liquid smoke, 2 t. garlic powder, 1 T. dried parsley and bring to a boil covered. Reduce heat and let simmer 1 hour. Serve with the stock, mustard and a pickle. Count as 3 carb grams per serving if prepared as above and the vegetables are consumed.

Makes about 4 servings.

Philly Cheese Steak

quantity	ingredient	carb grams
1 lb.	thinly sliced deli roast beef, coarse julienned	
1/2	medium onion, sliced	8
4 T.	olive oil	
1 t.	garlic powder	2
1/8 c.	water or dry red wine	1
6 oz.	provolone or mozzarella cheese	6
1	bouillon cube	1
	bell pepper (optional)	
	mushrooms (optional)	
	hot peppers (optional)	
	Total Carbohydrate Grams	18
	Carbohydrate Grams per serving	9.0

Method of Preparation:

Heat your non-stick skillet over medium high heat. Add 2 T. oil and your beef and cook until the meat is cooking well (in other words, you want to do more than just heat it up). Remove meat to a plate. In the same skillet over medium heat, add the remaining oil and the onion. You are going to cook the onions until they are beginning to brown. It is at this point that you add the optional ingredients and begin to cook them. Add the beef back in along with the water, the garlic powder and the bouillon cube, stir and bring to a boil. Let simmer covered about 5 minutes. Add the cheese, cover and let simmer an additional two minutes. Stir again, cover and let simmer still another two minutes. If you add any of the optional ingredients, do not forget to account for the increase in carbs.

Makes 2 servings.

One Skillet Chili Rellenos

You can use any kinds of peppers you want so you can provide as much spice to this as you want.

quantity	ingredient	carb grams
1 lb.	good hamburger	
3 oz.	American cheese	1.5
3 oz.	mozzarella cheese	1.5
2	medium bell peppers, sliced	12
1	medium onion, sliced	16
1/4 c.	water	
1	bouillon cube	1
1 T.	chili powder	1
2 t.	garlic powder	4
	Total Carbohydrate Grams	37.0
	Carbohydrate Grams per serving	18.5

Method of Preparation:

In a skillet, brown the hamburger and onion. Add the water, the bouillon cube, the chili powder and the garlic powder, bring to a boil, reduce the heat and simmer 5 minutes. Stir, add the peppers, cover and simmer again about 5 minutes. Stir and add the cheese and simmer another 5 minutes. The object is to get the peppers just to the point where they are just starting to wilt a little.

Makes 2 servings.

Carne Asada

quantity	ingredient	carb grams
1 1/2 lb.	beef, sliced very thin	
1 1/2 t.	salt	
1/2 t.	black pepper	
3 T.	olive oil	
1/4	medium onion, sliced	4
2 T.	lime juice	2
1 t.	garlic powder	2
2 t.	chili powder	5
	Pickled Onions (p. 216) for serving	
	diced tomatoes for serving	
	pickled jalapeño peppers for serving	
	guacamole for serving	
	salsa (p. 236) for serving	
	Total Carbohydrate Grams	13
	Carbohydrate Grams per serving	6.5

Method of Preparation:

Mix everything except the oil in a bowl and let marinate for as long as possible, at least and hour, overnight if possible. To cook, heat the oil in the skillet on medium high heat. Coat the skillet well. Add the marinated beef and any marinade to the oil and cook quickly to desired doneness. Serve with side dishes. Don't forget to account for the extra carbs in any of the side dishes.

Makes 2 servings.

Polish Style Beef

quantity	ingredient	carb grams
3 lb.	stew beef	
2 T.	olive oil	
1	medium onion, sliced	16
1/2 t.	black pepper	
1	bay leaf	
1 c.	water	
2	bouillon cube	2
2 oz.	dill pickles, diced	1
1 c.	sour cream	6
	Total Carbohydrate Grams	25
	Carbohydrate Grams per serving	4.2

Method of Preparation:

Brown the meat in the oil over medium high heat. Add the remaining ingredients except for the sour cream. Simmer for about 1 1/2 hours, stirring every half hour, until the meat is very tender. Stir in the sour cream. Serve with the sauce.

Makes about 6 servings.

Hint – One tablespoon is equivalent to 15 grams of water.

Barbecued Beef Short Ribs

quantity	ingredient	carb grams
6 lb.	beef short ribs, cut into pieces	
6	slices bacon, diced	
1/4 c.	onion, diced	4
1/4 c.	bell pepper, diced	3
2 c.	Ketchup (p. 219)	20
1 t.	salt	
2 t.	celery seed	1
1/4 c.	sugar equivalent sweetener	
1/4 c.	lemon juice	2
1 T.	dry mustard powder	1
1 c.	water	
2 t.	garlic powder	4
	Total Carbohydrate Grams	37
	Carbohydrate Grams per serving	6.2

Method of Preparation:

Cook the bacon over medium heat until it is well browned and crispy. Brown ribs. Mix remaining ingredients and pour over the ribs. Cover, bring to a boil, reduce heat and simmer covered for 2 hours stirring every half hour.

Makes about 6 servings.

Quick Beef Stroganoff

quantity	ingredient	carb grams
1 lb.	thin sliced deli roast beef, julienned	
8 oz.	canned mushrooms	10
1/2	medium onion, sliced	8
1/8 c.	dry white wine	1
1	bouillon cube	1
1 c.	sour cream	6
1 t.	dry mustard	1
4 t.	Ketchup (p. 219)	3
1 t.	garlic powder	2
1/2 t.	black pepper	
2 T.	olive oil	
	Total Carbohydrate Grams	32
	Carbohydrate Grams per serving	16.0

Method of Preparation:

Cook the onion in the oil over medium heat until it is clear. Add the beef and cook until it is cooking well. Add the wine, the mushrooms, the bouillon cube, the garlic, the pepper and the mustard, cover, bring to a boil, reduce the heat and simmer for about 5 minutes. Remove from the heat and add the sour cream and ketchup.

Makes 2 servings.

Hamburger Stroganoff

quantity	ingredient	carb grams
1 lb.	good hamburger	
4 oz.	canned mushroom stems (retain liquid)	5
1 c.	mushroom liquid plus water	
1/2 c.	onion, diced	8
2 t.	garlic powder	4
2	bouillon cubes	2
1/2 t.	black pepper	
1 c.	sour cream	6
4 T.	Ketchup (p. 219)	3
	Total Carbohydrate Grams	29
	Carbohydrate Grams per serving	14.5

Method of Preparation:

Cook and stir the meat and onion in a large skillet until the meat is brown. Add the bouillon, pepper, garlic, mushrooms and water and heat to boiling. Reduce the heat and simmer, covered, for 10 minutes. Stir in the sour cream, and turn off the heat.

Makes 2 servings.

Boef a la Stroganoff

quantity	ingredient	carb grams
2 lb.	filet mignon, diced in one inch cubes	
4 T.	olive oil	
1/2 c.	dry white wine	1
2 T.	tomato sauce	2
2 T.	Dijon mustard	
2	bouillon cubes	2
1	medium onion, sliced	16
1/2 lb.	button mushrooms, diced	8
1 c.	sour cream	6
1/2 t.	black pepper	
	Total Carbohydrate Grams	35
	Carbohydrate Grams per serving	8.8

Method of Preparation:

Heat 2 T. oil over medium high heat. Add the meat and pepper and cook ten minutes. Remove the meat. Add the remaining oil, the onions and the mushrooms and cook until the mushrooms are tender. Remove the onions and mushrooms. Over medium high heat, deglaze the pan with the wine, scraping the pan. Return the meat, the onions and the mushrooms to the pan. Add the bouillon cubes, the mustard and the tomato sauce and simmer uncovered about 5 minutes. Add the sour cream, remove from the heat and stir.

Makes about 4 servings.

Bul-Go-Gee

(Korean Bar-B-Q Beef)

quantity	ingredient	carb grams
1 lb.	beef roast, shaved and with fat removed	
2 t.	garlic powder	4
1	bunch scallions, diced	4
2 T.	sugar equivalent sweetener	
4 T.	soy sauce	
1 T.	sesame seeds	2
1/2 t.	black pepper	
1/4 t.	crushed red pepper	
2 T.	sesame oil	
1 t.	ginger	1
	Total Carbohydrate Grams	9
	Carbohydrate Grams per serving	4.5

Method of Preparation:

Julienne the scallions, then dice. Mix all ingredients well mixing the oil in last. Let sit one hour mixing every 15 minutes. Overnight is preferred. Can fry or broil but tastes best when cooked on a charcoal grill covered with aluminum foil with holes punched in it. If fried or broiled include a small, sliced onion

Makes 2 servings.

Kalbi

(Korean Bar-B-Q Ribs)

quantity	ingredient	carb grams
2-3 lb.	beef short ribs with fat removed	
2 t.	garlic powder	4
1	bunch scallions, diced	4
2 T.	sugar equivalent sweetener	
4 T.	soy sauce	
1 T.	sesame seeds	2
1/2 t.	black pepper	
1/4 t.	crushed red pepper	
2 T.	sesame oil	
1 t.	ginger	1
	Total Carbohydrate Grams	9
	Carbohydrate Grams per serving	4.5

Method of Preparation:

Mix all ingredients well in a bowl putting the oil in last. Let sit one hour stirring occasionally. Can bake or broil but tastes best if cooked over charcoal. Baste with the remaining liquid while cooking. Dip with Yaki Mandu Sauce (p. 233).

Makes 2 servings.

Italian Beef

quantity	ingredient	carb grams
2 lb.	stew beef	
4 T.	olive oil	
1/2 c.	dry red wine	1
1/4 c.	tomato sauce	3
1/2 lb.	button mushrooms	8
1	medium bell pepper, sliced	6
1/2	medium onion, sliced	8
1/4 c.	wine vinegar	
2 t.	Italian seasonings	2
2	bouillon cubes	2
1	whole bay leaf	
2 t.	garlic powder	4
	hot pepper sauce (optional)	
	Total Carbohydrate Grams	34
	Carbohydrate Grams per serving	8.5

Method of Preparation:

Brown the meat in the 2 T oil over medium high heat. Remove the meat. Add the remaining oil and cook the mushrooms, peppers, and onions until the mushrooms are tender. Add all other ingredients. Cover and bring to a boil. Reduce heat and simmer about an hour. Remove from heat and remove the bay leaf.

Makes about 4 servings.

Italian Beef *al la* Covelli

quantity	ingredient	carb grams
2 lb.	stew beef	
1/2 c.	dry red wine	1
1 1/2 c.	water	
1/2	medium onion, diced	8
2 t.	Italian seasonings	2
2	bouillon cubes	2
1	whole bay leaf	
2 t.	garlic powder	4
	Total Carbohydrate Grams	17
	Carbohydrate Grams per serving	4.3

Method of Preparation:

Place the onions, seasonings and bouillon cubes in a large pan. Place the beef in the pan. Add the liquids. Cover and bring to a boil. Reduce heat and simmer about an hour and a half stirring every 15 minutes. Remove from heat and remove the bay leaf. Let sit at least 15 minutes before serving. Serve with a half-cup of *au jus*.

Makes about 4 servings.

Bar-B-Q Brisket

quantity	ingredient	carb grams
4-5 lb.	brisket	
1	medium onion, sliced	16
2 c.	Bar-B-Q Sauce (p. 224)	20
1 t.	garlic powder	2
1 t.	salt	
1/2 t.	black pepper	
1/2 c.	water	
	Total Carbohydrate Grams	38
	Carbohydrate Grams per serving	6.3

Method of Preparation:

Preheat oven to 400 degrees. Trim visible fat off brisket (there is still plenty). Rub salt, pepper and garlic into brisket. Place onion in the bottom of your baking pan. Add the water. Place the brisket on top of the onion. Pour the Bar-B-Q Sauce evenly over the brisket. Bake at 400 degrees for 30 minutes. Reduce heat to 325 degrees and bake an additional 4 hours.

Makes about 6 servings.

Hint – One pint is equivalent to two cups.

Beef Brisket with Wine

quantity	ingredient	carb grams
4-5 lb.	brisket	
1	medium onion, sliced	16
2 c.	dry red wine	2
3 T.	lemon juice	2
2 t.	garlic powder	4
3	bouillon cubes	2
1/2 t.	black pepper	
1/2 c.	sugar equivalent sweetener	
	Total Carbohydrate Grams	26
	Carbohydrate Grams per serving	4.3

Method of Preparation:

Pre-heat oven to 400 degrees. Dissolve sweetener in wine and lemon juice. Trim visible fat off brisket (there is still plenty). Rub pepper and garlic into brisket. Place onion in the bottom of your baking pan. Place the brisket on top of the onion. Pour the wine and lemon juice over the brisket. Bake at 400 degrees for 30 minutes. Reduce heat to 325 degrees and bake an additional 4 hours.

Makes about 6 servings.

Texas Brisket

quantity	ingredient	carb grams
1	whole beef brisket, about six pounds	
1 c.	celery, diced	5
1	medium onion, sliced	16
2 c.	Chili Sauce (p. 220)	20
1	medium pepper, sliced	5
2 T.	Sliced, pickled jalapeño peppers	2
2 t.	salt	
3 T.	sugar equivalent sweetener	
2 T.	liquid smoke	
1/2 t.	allspice	
1/2 t.	five spice powder	
2 T.	paprika	6
2 T.	garlic powder	12
1/4 c.	cider vinegar	
	Total Carbohydrate Grams	66
	Carbohydrate Grams per serving	6.6

Method of Preparation:

Mix salt, sweetener, liquid smoke, allspice, five spice powder, paprika, garlic powder and vinegar into a paste. Rub this into the brisket and let sit for two hours.

Put the celery, onion and about one half of the peppers and one cup of Chili Sauce (p. 220) in a roasting pan and stir. Set the brisket in and pour over the remaining Chili Sauce and peppers. Bake at 350 degrees for an hour, reduce heat to 225 degrees and cook another six to eight hours or until the meat is tender. Slice and serve with some sauce and Bar-B-Q slaw (p. 31).

Makes about 10 servings.

Canadian Brisket

quantity	ingredient	carb grams
5 lb.	brisket or beef roast	
1	medium onion, sliced	16
1	medium carrot, diced	7
2	stalks celery, diced	3
1 c.	Chili Sauce (p. 220)	10
2 c.	water	
1 t.	salt	
1/2 t.	pepper	
1 t.	garlic powder	2
2 t.	dried parsley	
	Total Carbohydrate Grams	38
	Carbohydrate Grams per serving	4.8

Method of Preparation:

Remove most of the visible fat from the brisket (there is still plenty remaining). Place the brisket in your baking pan. Sprinkle with salt, pepper, garlic powder and parsley. Spread the vegetables around the meat and add the water. Cover the brisket with the chili sauce. Preheat oven to 400 degrees. Bake for one half-hour. Reduce heat and bake at 325 degrees for 4. Let sit about 15 minutes before serving.

Makes about 8 servings.

Pot Roast

quantity	ingredient	carb grams
3 lb.	roast	
2 T.	olive oil	
1/2	medium onion, diced	8
1	medium carrot, diced	7
2	stalks celery, diced	3
2 t.	dried parsley	
2 t.	garlic powder	4
1	bay leaf	
2 t.	salt	
1/2 t.	pepper	
1/2 c.	dry red wine	1
1/2 t.	thyme	
1/4 t.	nutmeg	
2	cloves	
2 c.	water	
	Total Carbohydrate Grams	23
	Carbohydrate Grams per serving	4.6

Method of Preparation:

Sear the roast in the olive oil. Add the remaining ingredients, cover, and bring to a boil. Reduce heat and simmer about 4 hours. Serve with the *au jus* as a dip and perhaps some horseradish sauce.

Makes about 5 servings.

New England Boiled Dinner

quantity	ingredient	carb grams
4 lb.	beef roast	
1	medium onion, sliced	16
1	medium carrot, sliced	7
2	stalks celery, sliced	3
2 lb.	cabbage cut into 8ths	36
1 T.	dried parsley	
2 t.	garlic powder	4
2 t.	salt	
1/2 t.	black pepper	
3 c.	water	
	Total Carbohydrate Grams	66
	Carbohydrate Grams per serving	9.4

Method of Preparation:

Place every thing in a large pan. Cover and bring to a boil. Reduce heat and simmer 2-3 hours.

Makes 7 servings.

German Style Beef

This recipe is an "easy" German Beef Rouladen recipe.

quantity	ingredient	carb grams
2 lb.	stew beef	
6	slices of bacon, diced	
1/2 t.	black pepper	
2 t.	garlic powder	4
1	medium onion, sliced	16
4 oz.	dill pickle, sliced thinly (lengthwise if possible)	2
1/2 c.	dry red wine	1
1 c.	water	
2	bouillon cubes	2
1/2 c.	Dijon mustard	
1/4 c.	prepared horseradish (very optional)	
	Total Carbohydrate Grams	25
	Carbohydrate Grams per serving	6.3

Method of Preparation:

Cook the bacon over medium heat until well browned. Remove the cooked bacon reserving as much of the grease as possible. Add the beef to the fat and fry until it is well browned on all sides. Add the onion and cook until it is clear. Return the bacon to the skillet and add the liquids, the spices and the bouillon cube. Cover, bring to a boil and let simmer covered about an hour, stirring every 15 minutes. Add the remaining ingredients and simmer uncovered until the amount of liquid is reduced to about 1 1/2 cups. Let sit about 10 minutes before serving. Serve with the sauce.

Makes 4 servings.

Sauerbraten

quantity	ingredient	carb grams
4 lb.	beef roast	
1 c.	vinegar	
2 c.	water	
1 1/2 t.	salt	
10	peppercorns, crushed	
1	medium onion, sliced	16
2	bay leaves	
4 T.	Pickling spices	
1 T.	garlic powder	6
2 T.	olive oil	
1 t.	ginger	1
1/2 c.	sour cream	3
2 t.	caraway seeds	2
1/4 c.	sugar equivalent sweetener	
	Total Carbohydrate Grams	28
	Carbohydrate Grams per serving	4.0

Method of Preparation:

In a saucepan bring the vinegar, water and salt to a boil. Remove from the heat and add the peppercorns, onion, bay leaves, garlic, ginger, caraway seeds, sweetener and pickling spices. Let cool to room temperature. Mix with the beef, cover, and refrigerate for 2 days, turning at least twice a day. When ready to cook, preheat the oven to 400 degrees. Remove the roast from the marinade and pat it dry with paper towels. Strain the marinade and reserve. Fry the roast in the oil in your roasting pan over medium high heat until it turns gray and begins to brown slightly. Pour the marinade over the meat, cover and cook 15 minutes. Reduce heat to 325 degrees and cook 2 1/2 - 3 hours, or until tender. Remove the roast from the stock. Slice the meat and serve with side dishes of stock and sour cream.

Makes 7 servings.

Beef Bourguignon

quantity	ingredient	carb grams
4 lb.	stew beef	
6	slices bacon, diced	
1 1/2 c.	red wine	1
1/4 c.	olive oil	
1 t.	thyme	
1 t.	black pepper	
2	bouillon cubes	2
2 t.	garlic powder	4
1	medium onion, diced	16
1 lb.	fresh mushrooms, sliced	16
	Total Carbohydrate Grams	39
	Carbohydrate Grams per serving	4.9

Method of Preparation:

In a bowl, mix the beef, wine, oil, thyme, pepper and garlic powder and let sit 4 hours at room temperature or overnight in the refrigerator if possible. In your large skillet, cook the bacon over medium heat until browned well. Add the onion, cooking until it becomes clear. Add the mushrooms and cook until they begin to wilt. Place the remaining ingredients in the pan, cover, bring to a boil, reduce the heat and simmer 1 1/2 hours stirring every 15 minutes.

Makes 8 servings.

Steak Diane

quantity	ingredient	carb grams
2	filet mignon steaks	
	salt and black pepper to taste	
2 T.	butter	
2 T.	olive oil	
1 t.	Dijon mustard	
4 t.	shallots	2
2 T.	Worcestershire Sauce (p. 222)	
2 T.	fresh lemon juice	2
	Total Carbohydrate Grams	4
	Carbohydrate Grams per serving	2

Method of Preparation:

Pound the steaks with a meat mallet between wax paper until they are 1/2-inch thickness. Sprinkle both sides with salt and pepper. Heat the skillet on the stove over medium high heat. Add 1 T. butter and the olive oil. When the butter sizzles, add the steaks and cook on both sides until they are done. Remove the steaks and keep warm. Add the remaining butter and sauté the shallots for a minute, add the Worcestershire Sauce and lemon juice and reduce the volume to about half. Pour over the steaks.

Makes 2 servings.

Grilled Beef Thai Style

This is not very hot, despite how it looks.

quantity	ingredient	carb grams
1.5 lb.	flank steak, sliced	
2	green chilies, diced	1
1/4 c.	white vinegar	
1/2	medium red onion, sliced	8
1/4 c.	scallions, sliced	2
1 T.	lime juice	1
5 T.	lime juice	5
2 T.	Thai fish sauce	
1 t.	red pepper flakes	
1 t.	coriander	
1 t.	basil	
	Total Carbohydrate Grams	17
	Carbohydrate Grams per serving	8.5

Method of Preparation:

Marinate the steak in 2 T. white vinegar, 1 T. of lime juice, coriander, chilies and basil for at least and hour. Cook (grill, fry, broil, etc.) the beef to desired doneness and place it in a bowl. Add the onion and mix. Add the 5 T. lime juice, fish sauce and red pepper flakes and mix well.

Makes 2 servings.

Golubtsi
(Russian Cabbage Rolls)

quantity	ingredient	carb grams
	boiling salted water	
12	large cabbage leaves (more or less)	15
2 lb.	ground beef	
2 t.	salt	
1 t.	garlic powder	2
2	eggs beaten	1
1/2 t.	black pepper	
1	medium onion, diced finely	16
1 c.	canned beef broth	1
1 c.	tomato sauce	12
4 dollops	sour cream	3
	Total Carbohydrate Grams	50
	Carbohydrate Grams per serving	12.5

Method of Preparation:

Place the cabbage leaves in the boiling water until wilted. Cool the cabbage leaves in cold water. Mix thoroughly the meats, eggs, seasonings and onion. Use one cabbage leaf per roll. Place the leaf on a cutting board and cut the ribs in order to make the leaf lie flat. Fill each leaf with about 3 oz. of the meat mixture in the center. Roll up each leaf, tucking in the ends or using a toothpick to keep them from unrolling. Place the rolls seam side down on a plate in preparation for cooking. Bring the beef broth and the tomato sauce to a rolling boil. Place the cabbage rolls in the liquid one at a time, carefully in order to maintain them as rolls. Cover and bring to a boil again. Reduce the heat and simmer 30 minutes. Serve with the sauce and a dollop of sour cream.

Makes about 4 servings.

Hungarian Goulash

quantity	ingredient	carb grams
2 lb.	stew beef	
2 T.	olive oil	
3 T.	paprika	9
2 t.	garlic powder	4
1/2 t.	black pepper	
1	bay leaf	
1/2	medium onion, diced	8
1/2 c.	canned beef stock	1
1 c.	sour cream	6
	Total Carbohydrate Grams	28
	Carbohydrate Grams per serving	7.0

Method of Preparation:

Fry the beef in the oil over medium high heat until the beef begins to brown. Add the onions and cook until they become clear. Add the remaining ingredients except the sour cream, cover and bring to a boil. Reduce heat and simmer 1 hour. Serve with the sour cream

Makes 4 servings.

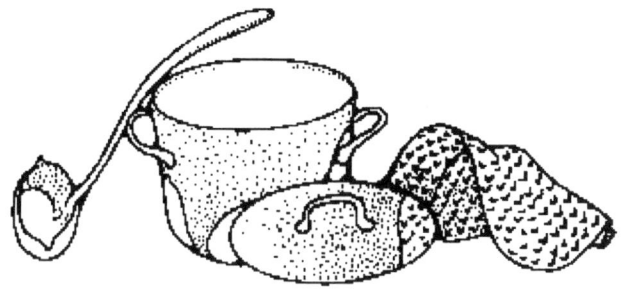

Spanish Meatloaf
suggested by Claudia Nelson

quantity	ingredient	carb grams
1 1/2 lb.	ground beef	
10	stuffed green olives, diced	5
1/4 c.	Ketchup (p. 219)	3
2	eggs beaten slightly	2
1/4	medium onion, diced	4
1 t.	garlic powder	2
1 t.	salt	
	Total Carbohydrate Grams	17
	Carbohydrate Grams per serving	5.7

Method of Preparation:

Mix all ingredients thoroughly. Bake 1 hour in a bread loaf pan in a 350-degree oven. You might want to reserve some of the ketchup for the top of the meatloaf.

Makes 3 servings.

Hint – One pint is equivalent to two cups.

Main Courses - Pork

Italian Roast Pork

quantity	ingredient	carb grams
4 lb.	boneless pork roast	
1/4 c.	dry white wine	1
1	bouillon cube	1
2 T.	dill weed	2
1 T.	fennel or anise seed	3
2 t.	Italian seasoning	2
2 T.	lemon juice	2
1 t.	onion powder	1
2 t.	garlic powder	4
1/2 t.	salt	
1 t.	pepper	
1/2 t.	cayenne pepper (optional)	
	Total Carbohydrate Grams	16
	Carbohydrate Grams per serving	2.7

Method of Preparation:

Combine seasonings with the lemon juice. Place the roast in a dutch oven or roasting pan. Pour the wine over it. Coat the roast evenly with the seasoning mixture. Cover and place in a pre-heated 400 degree oven for 15 minutes. Reduce heat to 325 degrees and continue baking for 1 1/2 hours. Let sit 15 minutes before serving.

Makes about 6 servings.

Oktoberfest Ribs

quantity	ingredient	carb grams
3 lb.	pork ribs	
1	can (15 oz.) sauerkraut	20
1/2	medium onion, sliced	8
12 oz.	low carb beer	3
2 T.	sugar equivalent sweetener	
1 t.	caraway seed	1
	Total Carbohydrate Grams	32
	Carbohydrate Grams per serving	8.0

Method of Preparation:

Rinse the kraut twice (see Sauerkraut Preparation p. 189). Mix the sweetener with the beer to ensure that it dissolves. In this order, place the kraut, onions and ribs in a pan. Pour the liquid over the ribs. Sprinkle the caraway seed over the roast. Cover and bring to a boil. Lower the heat and simmer very gently for 3 hours.

Makes about 4 serving.

Cajun Pork Roast

quantity	ingredient	carb grams
3 lb.	boneless pork roast	
1 T.	paprika	3
1 t.	cayenne pepper	1
2 t.	garlic powder	4
1 t.	oregano	1
1t.	thyme	
2 t.	salt	
1/2 t.	white pepper	
1 t.	black pepper	
1 t.	cumin	1
1/2 t.	nutmeg	
1 c.	water	
1	bouillon cube	1
	Total Carbohydrate Grams	11
	Carbohydrate Grams per serving	2.2

Method of Preparation:

Mix seasonings and rub well all over the roast. Pour the water in the roasting pan, add the bouillon cube and the roast and bake in a preheated 400 degree oven for 15 minutes. Reduce heat to 325 degrees and cook an additional hour and a half. Let sit 10 minutes before slicing.

Makes 5 servings.

Wisconsin Pork Stew

quantity	ingredient	carb grams
2 lb.	pork roast cut into one inch cubes	
2 t.	salt	
1/2 t.	black pepper	
2 T.	olive oil	
1/2	medium onion, sliced	8
1	medium carrot, sliced	7
2	stalks celery, sliced	3
2 t.	garlic powder	4
2 T.	dried parsley	
1 t.	caraway seed	1
1	bay leaf	
1	can (16 oz.) chicken stock	2
1	can (12 oz.) low carb beer	3
2 T.	malt vinegar	
1 T.	sugar equivalent sweetener	
	Total Carbohydrate Grams	28
	Carbohydrate Grams per serving	7.0

Method of Preparation:

In your soup pot, brown the meat in the oil over medium high heat. Add the vegetable and cook until the onions become clear. Add remaining ingredients, cover, bring to a boil and simmer an hour and a half stirring every 20 minutes. Let sit 5 minutes before serving.

Makes 4 servings.

Chinese Style Pork Burgers

quantity	ingredient	carb grams
1 1/2 lb.	ground pork	
1	egg, beaten	1
2 T.	soy sauce	
2 T.	sugar equivalent sweetener	
1/2 t.	ginger	
2 t.	garlic powder	4
1 t.	onion powder	1
1/2 t.	hot pepper flakes	
2 t.	sesame oil	
	Total Carbohydrate Grams	6
	Carbohydrate Grams per serving	1.0

Method of Preparation:

Mix thoroughly all ingredients. Form into 4 oz. patties and fry over medium heat.

Makes 6 servings.

Danish Style Cabbage Rolls

quantity	ingredient	carb grams
	boiling salted water	
1	large head cabbage, cored	15
1 lb.	ground pork	
1 lb.	ground veal	
2 t.	salt	
2	eggs beaten	2
1/2 t.	black pepper	
1/2	medium onion, diced finely	8
2 c.	canned beef broth	2
3 T.	sugar equivalent sweetener	
	Total Carbohydrate Grams	27
	Carbohydrate Grams per serving	6.8

Method of Preparation:

Preheat the oven to 375 degrees. Place the head of cabbage in the boiling water to loosen the leaves, about 15 minutes. Cool the cabbage in cold water. Mix thoroughly the meats, eggs, seasonings and onion. Use one cabbage leaf per roll. Place the leaf on a cutting board and cut the ribs in order to make the leaf lie flat. Fill each leaf with a tablespoon of the meat mixture in the center. Roll up each leaf, tucking in the ends or using a toothpick to keep them from unrolling. Place the rolls seam side down in your baking dish. Combine the sweetener with the broth and pour over the rolls. Bake uncovered for 30 minutes. Turn the rolls over and bake another 30 minutes.

Makes about 4 servings.

German Meatballs

quantity	ingredient	carb grams
1/2	medium onion, diced	8
2 T.	butter	
1 1/2 lb.	lean ground pork	
1/2 lb.	ground beef	
1/4 c.	half and half	2
2	eggs beaten slightly	2
1	can (3 oz.) sardines, diced	
2 t.	salt	
1/4 t.	white pepper	
1 t.	garlic powder	2
1	can (15 oz.) chicken stock	2
2 oz.	Capers, drained	
1/4 c.	white wine vinegar	
	Total Carbohydrate Grams	16
	Carbohydrate Grams per serving	4.0

Method of Preparation:

Fry the onions in the butter over medium heat until they are clear. Remove from the heat and let cool. Mix the onions well with the pork, beef, garlic, half and half, eggs, 3/4 of the sardines, salt and pepper. Roll in 2 inch meat balls and let sit about 15 minutes in the refrigerator. When you are ready to cook, bring the chicken stock, vinegar, capers and remaining sardines to a rolling boil over high heat in a large pan. Remove the meatballs from the refrigerator and drop them into the sauce. Cover, bring to a boil again, and let simmer covered 20 minutes. Serve with a small bowl of the sauce for dipping.

Makes 4 servings.

Grilled Javanese Pork Sate

quantity	ingredient	carb grams
1 lb.	boneless pork roast, cut in 1/2 inch cubes	
2 T	smooth peanut butter	6
1/2 c.	onion, diced	8
2 T.	lemon juice	2
2 T.	soy sauce	
1 t.	garlic powder	2
1 T.	sugar equivalent sweetener	
1/4 t.	hot pepper sauce	
1 T.	peanut oil	
	Total Carbohydrate Grams	18
	Carbohydrate Grams per serving	9.0

Method of Preparation:

Mix all of the liquids and dissolve the sweetener in it. Add the onion and let sit 15 minutes. Slowly blend this mixture in with the peanut butter and 1 T. peanut oil. When it is well mixed, add the pork and mix thoroughly. Marinate several hours, overnight if possible, stirring occasionally. Put the pork on skewers and cook over hot coals until well done, 10 minutes, turning every couple of minutes.

Makes 2 servings.

Pork and Shrimp Cakes

quantity	ingredient	carb grams
8 oz.	salad shrimp (2 cans very small shrimp, reserve the juice)	
8 oz.	lean ground pork	
1 T.	sherry	1
1 T.	soy sauce	
1/4 t.	pepper	
1 t.	garlic powder	2
1 t.	onion powder	1
1 T.	sesame oil	
4	scallions, diced well	2
1	medium egg	1
4 T.	cooking oil	
	Total Carbohydrate Grams	7
	Carbohydrate Grams per serving	2.3

Method of Preparation:

Mix all ingredients, except the oil, along with 3 T. of the juice from the shrimp. Let sit at least ten minutes. Heat your skillet over medium heat and add 2 T. oil. Divide the mixture into six equal parts. Cook well-flattened patties in oil with lid over medium low heat. Patties are cooked when they are well browned on both sides. Serve with soy sauce or Mandu Sauce.

Makes three servings.

Eastern North Carolina Style Bar-B-Q

This regional delicacy cooks the meat twice. First you smoke it until it's done, or about done, then you boil it in a vinegar based Bar-B-Q sauce to complete the cooking. Serve with Bar-B-Q Slaw (p. 31) or Eastern Carolina Slaw (p. 33).

quantity	ingredient	carb grams
1	six pound shoulder roast or Boston butt roast	
1/2 qt.	water	
1/2 qt.	cider vinegar	
2 T.	dried red pepper flakes	1
1 T.	garlic powder	6
1 T.	onion powder	3
1 T.	salt	
	Total Carbohydrate Grams	10
	Carbohydrate Grams per serving	1.3

Method of Preparation:

Smoke the meat according to the instructions that came with your smoker, trying to keep the temperature between 220-240 degrees Fahrenheit. Smoking should last between 8-10 hours or until the meat comes easily away from the bone. During the last few hours you can gradually increase the temperature to 300 degrees. If it becomes too dark outside to continue the smoking, go ahead and remove the meat to a large pan (which you can cover with a lid), add the remaining ingredients, bring to a boil, and let simmer covered until the meat is well separated from the bone. If it becomes too late, you can just turn this off and continue it the next day without worrying about refrigeration.

Makes about 8 servings.

Twice Cooked Pork and Cabbage

quantity	ingredient	carb grams
1/4 lb.	cooked pork roast, sliced bite-size	
1/4 lb.	cabbage, sliced bite-size	5
1/2	medium onion, sliced	8
1 t.	powder	2
1/2 t.	red pepper flakes	
2 T.	olive oil	
2 t.	soy sauce	
1 T.	vinegar	
1/4 c.	pork or chicken stock	
1 t.	sugar equivalent sweetener	
	Total Carbohydrate Grams	15
	Carbohydrate Grams per serving	15

Method of Preparation:

Over medium-high heat, cook the pork in 1 T. of oil. The pork should be cooking and not just heated. Remove the pork to a bowl leaving as much oil in the skillet as possible. Add the remaining oil and the onion and cook until the onion is clear, stirring every couple of minutes. Add the cabbage and the red pepper flakes and cook until the cabbage begins to wilt, stirring every couple of minutes. Add everything else and simmer uncovered about 5 minutes, stirring every couple of minutes.

Makes 1 serving.

Bar-B-Q Pork Ribs (1)

This is our basic rib recipe. Others, more involved, follow.

quantity	ingredient	carb grams
2 1/2 lb.	country style pork ribs	
1 c.	Bar-B-Q Sauce (p. 224)	10
	Total Carbohydrate Grams	10
	Carbohydrate Grams per serving	2.5

Method of Preparation:

Place ribs in a pan. Cover with water, bring to a boil, reduce heat and simmer 30 minutes. Drain the ribs. Place ribs in a low baking dish, then cover with the Bar-B-Q Sauce and bake 30 minutes at 325 degrees. Stir, making sure to coat ribs and bake another 30 minutes. Stir a final time and bake a final 30 minutes.

Makes about 4 servings.

Hint – One cup of water is equivalent to eight ounces.

Bar-B-Q Pork Ribs (2)

quantity	ingredient	carb grams
2 1/2 lb.	country style pork ribs	
1/4 c.	soy sauce	
3 T.	cider vinegar	
1 t.	garlic powder	2
1/2 c.	onions, chopped	8
2 T.	cooking oil	
1/4 c.	sugar equivalent sweetener	
10 oz.	tomato sauce	15
1 T.	jalapeño peppers, diced	1
	Total Carbohydrate Grams	31
	Carbohydrate Grams per serving	7.8

Method of Preparation:

Place ribs in a pan. Cover with water, bring to a boil, reduce heat and simmer 30 minutes. Drain the ribs. In the meantime, start the sauce by frying the onion in the oil in a sauce pan over medium heat until the onions are clear. Add the tomato sauce, sweetener, soy sauce, vinegar and peppers. Simmer, stirring occasionally, for 30 minutes. Place ribs in a low baking dish, then cover with the sauce and bake at 325 degrees 30 minutes. Stir, making sure to coat ribs, and bake another 30 minutes. Stir a final time and bake a final 30 minutes.

Makes 4 servings.

Pork Chops Dijon

quantity	ingredient	carb grams
4	pork chops, about 1/2 inch thick	
2 T.	olive oil	
1/4	medium onion, diced	4
3 T.	Dijon mustard	
	salt and pepper to taste	
1/4 c.	Vinaigrette Dressing (p. 13)	2
	Total Carbohydrate Grams	6
	Carbohydrate Grams per serving	3.0

Method of Preparation:

Heat oil in skillet over medium heat. Add the pork chops and sprinkle with salt and pepper. Brown on both sides. Remove the chops from the skillet and cook the onions until they are clear. Replace the chops in the pan. Mix all other ingredients into a paste and pour it over the chops. Cover and cook over medium low heat 20 minutes until the meat is tender. Let rest 10 minutes before serving.

Makes 2 servings.

Rosemary Pork Chops

quantity	ingredient	carb grams
4	1 inch thick pork chops	
2 T.	butter	
1 T.	olive oil	
1 t.	rosemary	1
1 t.	sage	
1 t.	garlic powder	2
1 t.	onion powder	1
1/2 t.	salt	
1/4 t.	black pepper	
3/4 c.	dry white wine	1
	Total Carbohydrate Grams	5
	Carbohydrate Grams per serving	1.3

Method of Preparation:

Make a mixture of the seasonings and mash it into both sides of each pork chop. Fry the chops in the butter and oil over medium heat, browning on both sides. Add the wine, cover and bring to a boil. Reduce heat and simmer 30-45 minutes or until the chops are tender. Remove the chops from the skillet and reduce the sauce to a syrup which is then poured over the chops.

Makes 4 servings.

Pork and Kim-chee

quantity	ingredient	carb grams
1 lb.	shaved pork	
2 T.	sesame oil	
1 T.	sesame seeds	2
3 T.	sugar equivalent sweetener	
3 T.	soy sauce	
1/2 t.	ginger	
1 t.	garlic powder	2
1	bunch scallions, sliced	4
1/2	medium onion, sliced	8
1/2	medium carrot, shredded	4
1 c.	American cabbage kim-chee	10
	Total Carbohydrate Grams	30
	Carbohydrate Grams per serving	15.0

Method of Preparation:

Mix first seven ingredients and let marinade at least 30 minutes. In a heated skillet cook the meat in 1 tablespoon peanut oil over high heat. Add the remaining ingredients and continue cooking until the onions are clear.

Makes 2 servings.

Thai Pork Satay

(Thai style Bar-B-Q Pork)

quantity	ingredient	carb grams
1 lb.	boneless pork, cut into thin strips	
	Marinade Ingredients	
1 t.	garlic powder	2
1/4	medium onion, diced finely	4
1 T.	sugar equivalent sweetener	
2 T.	lime juice	2
1 T.	nam pla fish sauce	
1 T.	peanut oil	
	Sauce Ingredients	
4 T.	crunchy peanut butter	12
1/4	medium onion, diced finely	4
1/2 c.	Faux Coconut Milk (p. 238)	2
1 T.	sugar equivalent sweetener	
1/2 t.	cayenne pepper	
1 T.	dried lemon grass, chopped finely	1
2 t.	nam pla fish sauce	
2 t.	soy sauce	
	Total Carbohydrate Grams	27
	Carbohydrate Grams per serving	13.5

Method of Preparation:

Dissolve the sweetener in the lime juice. Combine with the remaining marinade ingredients; then add the meat and stir well. Marinate at least an hour, stirring every 20 minutes. To make the sauce, combine all of the sauce ingredients in a saucepan and heated to boiling temperature. Cook the pork strips on a grill. Serve the sauce in side bowls for dipping.

Makes 2 servings.

German Baked Pork Chops

quantity	ingredient	carb grams
6	pork chops	
1 t.	garlic powder	2
1 t.	onion powder	1
1 t.	caraway seeds	1
2 t.	paprika	2
1/2 t.	salt	
1/4 t.	black pepper	
1 c.	dry white wine	1
2 T.	white wine vinegar	
1 c.	sour cream	6
	Total Carbohydrate Grams	13
	Carbohydrate Grams per serving	4.3

Method of Preparation:

Prepare a marinade of everything except the pork chops and the sour cream. Marinate the pork chops in the marinade for several hours. Place the pork chops in a baking dish and pour the marinade over them. Bake uncovered at 325 degrees for an hour. Check every 15 minutes and add more wine if necessary. When the chops are finished, remove them from the pan. Ensure that you have at least a half cup of liquid (add more wine) and stir in the sour cream. Pour sauce over chops and serve.

Makes 3 servings.

Main Courses - Chicken

Basque Chicken

quantity	ingredient	carb grams
2	slices bacon, diced	
1 T.	olive oil	
1 lb.	boneless chicken, cut into 1/2 inch cubes	
1/2	medium onion, sliced	8
1	medium bell pepper, sliced	6
1 t.	sugar equivalent sweetener	
1 t.	garlic powder	2
4 oz.	ham, sliced	
2 oz.	dry white wine	1
2 T.	tomato sauce	3
1/2 t.	basil	
1/2 t.	dried parsley	
	Total Carbohydrate Grams	20
	Carbohydrate Grams per serving	10.0

Method of Preparation:

Fry the bacon over medium heat until the fat is rendered and the bacon is well browned. Remove the crisp bacon pieces reserving the fat. Add the oil. Brown the chicken over medium high heat. Remove the chicken reserving the oil. Add the onions and cook them until they begin to brown. Add the chicken, the bacon, the ham, the peppers and the garlic powder and cook over medium low heat until the chicken is done. Remove everything from the skillet and reserve. Deglaze the pan with the wine, add the sweetener, the tomato sauce, the basil and the parsley. Let simmer a couple of minutes. Spoon the sauce over the chicken and vegetables and serve.

Makes 2 servings.

Chicken St. Germain

quantity	ingredient	carb grams
2 lb.	boneless chicken, cut into 1/2 inch cubes	
4	slices bacon, diced	
1/4 c.	butter	
8 oz.	Mushrooms, cut in half	8
1/2	medium onion, diced	8
4	scallions, diced	2
2 t.	garlic powder	4
2 c.	chopped lettuce	3
1/2 c.	canned beef stock	
1/4 c.	tomato sauce	3
1 t.	soy sauce	
1 t.	sugar equivalent sweetener	
1/2 t.	black pepper	
1 t.	thyme	
1	bay leaf	
1 T.	dried parsley	
	Total Carbohydrate Grams	28
	Carbohydrate Grams per serving	7.0

Method of Preparation:

Fry the bacon over medium heat until it is well browned. Add the butter and let it melt. Increase the temperature to medium high and fry the chicken until it begins to brown. Add the onions and scallions and cook until the onions begin to clear. Add the mushrooms and lettuce and cook until the mushrooms begin to wilt slightly. Add remaining ingredients, cover and bring to a boil. Reduce heat and simmer 45 minutes. Let sit 5 minutes before serving.

Makes 4 servings.

Chicken Sauté Grandmere

quantity	ingredient	carb grams
2 lb.	boneless chicken, cut into 1/2 inch cubes	
4	slices bacon, diced	
1/4 c.	butter	
1/2	medium onion, diced	8
2 t.	garlic powder	4
1 1/4 c.	diced ham or smoked polish sausage	
1/2	green pepper, diced	3
2	stalks celery, diced	3
1/2 t.	black pepper	
1/2 c.	canned chicken stock	
2 T.	dried parsley	
	Total Carbohydrate Grams	18
	Carbohydrate Grams per serving	4.5

Method of Preparation:

Fry the bacon over medium heat until it is well browned. Add the butter and let it melt. Increase the temperature to medium high and fry the chicken until it begins to brown. Add the onions and cook until the onions begin to clear. Add remaining ingredients, cover and bring to a boil. Reduce heat and simmer 45 minutes.

Makes 4 servings.

Chicken Diablo

quantity	ingredient	carb grams
2 lb.	boneless chicken, cut in 1/2 inch cubes	
2 T.	olive oil	
1/4	medium onion, sliced	4
1	medium bell pepper, sliced	6
1/2 c.	water	
1/4 c.	dry red wine	1
2 t.	garlic powder	4
1 t.	salt	
2 T.	Faux Balsamic Vinegar (p. 223)	
1/2 t.	black pepper	
1 t.	cayenne pepper	1
4 T.	tomato sauce	3
2 t.	Italian seasoning	1
	Total Carbohydrate Grams	20
	Carbohydrate Grams per serving	5.0

Method of Preparation:

Fry the chicken in the oil over medium high heat until it begins to brown. Add the onions and cook until they are clear. Add the remaining ingredients, cover and bring to a boil. Reduce the heat and simmer 45 minutes. Remove the lid and reduce the sauce to about 1/2 cup.

Makes 4 servings.

Pepperoni Chicken

quantity	ingredient	carb grams
2 lb.	boneless chicken, cut into 1/2 inch cubes	
2 t.	olive oil	
1/4 lb.	pepperoni, sliced	
1/2	bell pepper, diced	3
1/4	medium onion, diced	4
4 oz.	black olives	4
2 t.	garlic powder	4
1 t.	anise or fennel	1
2	bouillon cube	2
1/2 t.	pepper	
1/2 c.	dry white wine	1
1 c.	shredded mozzarella cheese	4
1/2 c.	Parmesan cheese	2
	Total Carbohydrate Grams	25
	Carbohydrate Grams per serving	6.3

Method of Preparation:

In an ovenproof skillet, fry the chicken in the oil over medium high head until it begins to brown slightly. Add the onions and cook until they begin to clear. Add the remaining ingredients except the pepperoni and cheese, cover and bring to a boil. Reduce heat and simmer 45 minutes. After 45 minutes, turn on the oven broiler. Remove the lid and stir in the pepperoni. Sprinkle the Parmesan cheese over the contents of the skillet then the mozzarella and put under the broiler until the cheese browns.

Makes 4 servings.

Chicken and Sausage

quantity	ingredient	carb grams
2 lb.	boneless chicken cut into 1/2 inch cubes	
1/2 lb.	smoked polish sausage, sliced	8
1/2	medium onion, sliced	8
2 T.	olive oil	
1 T.	garlic powder	6
1/4 c.	soy sauce	
1 c.	canned chicken broth	1
	Total Carbohydrate Grams	23
	Carbohydrate Grams per serving	5.8

Method of Preparation:

Marinate the chicken in the soy sauce for an hour or longer, overnight if possible. Fry the chicken over medium high heat until it becomes gray and begins to brown slightly. Add the onion and polish sausage and cook until the onion begins to clear. Add the chicken broth and garlic powder, cover and bring to a boil. Reduce the heat and simmer 45 minutes. Let sit 5 minutes before serving.

Makes 4 servings.

Chicken in Riesling

quantity	ingredient	carb grams
2 lb.	boneless chicken, cut into 1/2 inch cubes	
2 1/2 oz.	butter	
1	bouillon cube	1
1/2 t.	pepper	
1/4	medium onion, diced	4
2 t.	garlic powder	4
5 oz.	fresh mushrooms, cut in half	5
1 c.	Riesling wine	1
3 T.	heavy cream	3
	Total Carbohydrate Grams	18
	Carbohydrate Grams per serving	4.5

Method of Preparation:

Fry the chicken in the butter over medium high heat until it begins to brown slightly. Add the onion and cook until it becomes clear. Add the remaining ingredients except the cream, cover and bring to a boil. Reduce heat and simmer 45 minutes. Remove the lid and reduce the sauce to half a cup and blend in the cream. Serve the chicken with the sauce.

Makes 4 servings.

Lemon Tomato Chicken

quantity	ingredient	carb grams
2 lb.	boneless chicken, cut in 1/2 inch cubes	
2 T.	lemon juice	2
2 t.	dried rosemary	1
3 oz.	dried tomatoes in oil, diced	23
2 T.	dry white wine	1
2 t.	garlic powder	4
1 t.	onion powder	1
1/2 t.	salt	
	Total Carbohydrate Grams	32
	Carbohydrate Grams per serving	8.0

Method of Preparation:

Combine all ingredients except the tomatoes, mix well and let marinate for an hour. Preheat the oven to 400 degrees. Mix the tomatoes in with the marinade, place in a casserole dish, and bake 15 minutes. Reduce heat to 325 degrees and bake an additional 45 minutes.

Makes 4 servings.

Hint – Watch for hidden carbs in medications and supplements. Look especially for things like maltodextrin.

Burgundy Chicken

quantity	ingredient	carb grams
2 lb.	boneless chicken, cut into 1/2 inch cubes	
2 T.	olive oil	
2 t.	garlic powder	4
1/4	medium onion, diced	4
8 oz.	fresh mushrooms, cut in half	8
1 c.	dry red wine	1
1	bouillon cube	1
	Total Carbohydrate Grams	18
	Carbohydrate Grams per serving	4.5

Method of Preparation:

Fry the chicken in the oil over medium high heat until it begins to brown slightly. Add the onions and cook until the onions become clear. Add the mushrooms and cook until they begin to wilt slightly. Add the remaining ingredients, cover and bring to a boil. Reduce heat and simmer 45 minutes stirring at least once.

Makes 4 servings.

Chicken Bordeaux

quantity	ingredient	carb grams
2 lb.	boneless chicken, cut into 1/2 inch cubes	
2 T.	olive oil	
2 t.	garlic powder	4
1/4	medium onion, diced	4
8 oz.	fresh mushrooms, cut in half	8
1 c.	dry white bordeaux wine	1
2 t.	sugar equivalent sweetener	
1/4 c.	tomato sauce	3
1	bouillon cube	1
1/2 t.	black pepper	
	Total Carbohydrate Grams	21
	Carbohydrate Grams per serving	5.3

Method of Preparation:

Fry the chicken in the oil over medium high heat until it begins to brown slightly. Add the onions and cook until the onions become clear. Add the mushrooms and cook until they begin to wilt slightly. Add the remaining ingredients, cover and bring to a boil. Reduce heat and simmer 45 minutes stirring at least once. Let sit 5 minutes before serving.

Makes 4 servings.

Chicken Vinaigrette

quantity	ingredient	carb grams
2 lb.	boneless chicken, cut into 1/2 inch cubes	
2 t.	garlic powder	4
1/2 t.	salt	
1/2 t.	cloves	
1 t.	cinnamon	1
1	bay leaf	
1/2 t.	black pepper	
2 T.	olive oil	
1/2	medium onion, sliced	8
1/4 c.	green olives	2
2 T.	red wine vinegar	
2 T.	dry red wine	1
1 T.	lemon juice	1
1 T.	sugar equivalent sweetener	
	Total Carbohydrate Grams	14
	Carbohydrate Grams per serving	3.5

Method of Preparation:

Fry the chicken over medium high heat until it begins to brown. Add the remaining ingredients, cover, and bring to a boil. Reduce heat and simmer 45 minutes. Remove from the heat and remove the bay leaf.

Makes 4 servings.

Chicken Jalfrezi

quantity	ingredient	carb grams
2 lb.	boneless chicken, cut into 1/2 inch cubes	
2 T.	olive oil	
1/2	medium onion, diced	8
1	medium bell pepper, sliced	6
2 t.	cumin	2
1 t.	ginger	1
1/2 c.	tomato sauce	6
1/2 c.	water	
1	bouillon cube	1
4 T.	hot curry paste	4
	Total Carbohydrate Grams	28
	Carbohydrate Grams per serving	7.0

Method of Preparation:

Fry chicken in oil over medium high heat until it begins to brown slightly. Add onions and cumin and cook until the onions clear. Add the remaining ingredients, cover and bring to a boil. Reduce heat and simmer 45 minutes. Let sit 5 minutes before serving.

Makes 4 servings.

Chicken Divan

quantity	ingredient	carb grams
2 lb.	boneless chicken breasts, cut in 1/2 inch cubes	
3 T.	butter	
1 c.	canned chicken broth	1
1 lb.	fresh broccoli florets	16
1/4	medium onion, diced	4
1/4 c.	dry white wine	1
1/4 c.	Parmesan	1
1/2 c.	whipping cream	3
	Total Carbohydrate Grams	26
	Carbohydrate Grams per serving	6.5

Method of Preparation:

Cook the chicken breasts in the butter over medium high heat until it begins to brown. Add the onion and cook until it is clear. Add the wine and the chicken broth, cover and bring to a boil. Reduce heat and simmer 45 minutes. Add the whipping cream and the Parmesan and stir until the Parmesan is incorporated into the cream. It will thicken slightly. Place the broccoli in a baking dish and pour the chicken mixture over it. Sprinkle with more Parmesan cheese and bake at 350 degrees for 20 minutes.

Makes 4 servings.

Bengali Chicken

quantity	ingredient	carb grams
2 lb.	boneless chicken, cut into 1/2 inch cubes	
1/2	medium onion, sliced	8
2 T.	olive oil	
2	bay leaves	
1 t.	cinnamon	1
1 t.	clove	1
1/2 t.	turmeric	
2 T.	chili powder	6
1	bouillon cube	1
1/2 c.	tomato sauce	6
1/2 c.	water	
	Total Carbohydrate Grams	23
	Carbohydrate Grams per serving	5.8

Method of Preparation:

Fry chicken in oil over medium high heat until the chicken begins to brown. Add the onions and the seasonings and cook until they become clear. Add the liquids and the bouillon cube, cover and bring to a boil. Reduce the heat and simmer 45 minutes. Remove the bay leaves. Let sit 10 minutes before serving.

Makes 4 servings.

Grecian Chicken

quantity	ingredient	carb grams
2 lb.	boneless chicken breasts, cut into 1/2 inch cubes	
2 T.	olive oil	
1 t.	ground cumin	1
1 t.	ground coriander	
1 t.	basil	1
1/2	turmeric	
1/2 t.	dried mint	
1 t.	onion powder	1
1 t.	garlic powder	2
1/4 c.	lime juice	2
1/4 c.	water	
1	bouillon cube	1
	Total Carbohydrate Grams	8
	Carbohydrate Grams per serving	2.0

Method of Preparation:

Marinate the chicken, seasonings and lime juice for at least an hour stirring occasionally. Cook the chicken in the oil over medium high heat until it becomes gray and begins to brown slightly. Add the water and the bouillon cube, cover and bring to a boil. Reduce heat and simmer for 45 minutes.

Makes 4 servings.

Thai Grilled Chicken

quantity	ingredient	carb grams
2 lb.	boneless chicken breast, sliced	
1 c.	Faux Coconut Milk (p. 238)	3
2 t.	garlic powder	4
2 T.	pickled jalapeño peppers, diced	2
2 t.	ginger	2
3 T.	soy sauce	
1 T.	lime zest	1
4 T.	lime juice	4
2 T.	sugar equivalent sweetener	
2 t.	coriander	1
	Total Carbohydrate Grams	17
	Carbohydrate Grams per serving	4.3

Method of Preparation:

Combine all ingredients except the chicken. Take 1/2 cup of the mixture and combine with the chicken. Let marinate at least an hour. Grill the chicken until it is thoroughly cooked. Heat the remaining sauce almost to boiling and serve in side bowls for dipping.

Makes 4 servings.

Hint – Because low carb diets tend to be diuretic, you need to drink at least a half gallon of water per day.

20 Cloves of Garlic Chicken

quantity	ingredient	carb grams
3 lb.	fryer cut into pieces	
2 T.	oil	
20	cloves garlic peeled	20
1/2 c.	dry white wine	1
1/2 c.	canned chicken stock	1
1/2 c.	whipping cream	3
1 t.	onion powder	1
	salt and pepper to taste	
	Total Carbohydrate Grams	26
	Carbohydrate Grams per serving	8.7

Method of Preparation:

Spread the garlic cloves in the bottom of a dutch oven. Pour the wine and oil over the garlic and sprinkle it lightly with salt. Place the chicken on top of the garlic and sprinkle with salt, pepper and onion powder. Bake 45 minutes in a preheated 400 degree oven, or until the dark meat comes off the bone. Return the pan to the top of the stove. Remove the chicken from the pan. Add the chicken stock and the cream and bring to a boil. Let reduce uncovered 3 minutes.

Makes 3 servings.

Mu Shu Chicken

quantity	ingredient	carb grams
1 lb.	boneless chicken, diced	
2	Eggs, already scrambled and set aside	1
2 T.	peanut oil	
1/2	medium onion, sliced	8
2 t.	ginger	2
1 t.	garlic powder	2
2 c.	cabbage, sliced	10
1/2	medium bell pepper, sliced	3
2 oz.	large mushrooms, sliced	2
2 c.	bean sprouts	12
1/2 c.	bamboo shoots, julienne	2
2 T.	soy sauce	
2 t.	sugar equivalent sweetener	
	Total Carbohydrate Grams	42
	Carbohydrate Grams per serving	21.0

Method of Preparation:

Dissolve the sweetener in the soy sauce. Fry the chicken in the oil over medium high heat until it begins to brown. Add the cabbage, the ginger and the garlic and cook until the cabbage begins to wilt. Add the onions and cook until they become clear. Add the bell pepper, mushrooms, bamboo shoots and soy sauce and cook until the mushrooms begin to wilt. Add the remaining ingredients and cook another 2 minutes.

Makes 2 servings.

Chicken Breasts With Mushrooms

quantity	ingredient	carb grams
2 lb.	boneless chicken breasts, cut in 1/2 inch cubes	
2 T.	olive oil	
1/2	medium yellow onion, sliced	8
4	scallions, sliced	2
1 1/2 c.	sliced mushrooms	6
2 t.	garlic powder	4
1/2 t.	salt	
1/2 c.	dry white wine	1
	Total Carbohydrate Grams	21
	Carbohydrate Grams per serving	5.3

Method of Preparation:

Fry the chicken in the oil over medium high heat until it begins to brown. Add the onions and cook until the yellow onion becomes clear. Add the mushrooms, the salt and the garlic and cook until the mushrooms begin to wilt. Add the wine, cover and bring to a boil. Reduce heat and simmer 45 minutes.

Makes 4 servings.

Worcestershire Chicken

quantity	ingredient	carb grams
2 lb.	boneless chicken breast, cut into 1/2 inch cubes	
2 T.	olive oil	
1/2	medium onion, diced	8
2 t.	garlic powder	4
6 T.	Worcestershire Sauce (p. 222)	
1 T.	lemon juice	1
1/4 c.	dry wine	1
1/2 t.	black pepper	
	Total Carbohydrate Grams	14
	Carbohydrate Grams per serving	3.5

Method of Preparation:

Fry the chicken in the oil over medium high heat until the chicken begins to brown. Add the onions and cook until the onions become clear. Add the remaining ingredients, cover and bring to a boil. Reduce heat and simmer 45 minutes. Let sit 5 minutes before serving.

Makes 4 servings.

Hint – One quart of water is equivalent to 32 ounces.

Red-Cooked Chicken

Suggested by Barbara Pollack

quantity	ingredient	carb grams
5 lb.	chicken thighs	
1 c.	soy sauce	
1 c.	water	
1 T.	garlic powder	6
1 t.	ginger	1
1 t.	star anise	1
1 t.	sugar equivalent sweetener	
2	scallions, sliced	1
	Total Carbohydrate Grams	9
	Carbohydrate Grams per serving	1.8

Method of Preparation:

Red-cooking sauce is a Chinese master sauce. This means that it is saved between batches and reused, getting richer and richer each time. Combine all ingredients except chicken and bring to a boil. Optionally skin the chicken. Add the chicken and return to boiling. If you don't have enough liquid then just add more soy sauce and water. Cover and simmer for 30 minutes. Turn off heat and let stand for 20 minutes. The chicken is ready to serve. It also keeps in the refrigerator for several days. It is good hot or cold. After cooking just strain the sauce into a refrigerator container. Allow the fat to remain on top until just before reusing the sauce. To reuse remove the fat and throw it away and boil the sauce for 15 minutes (just a precaution against possible microbe growth) before adding the items to be cooked. Periodically add more seasonings and soy sauce.

Makes 5 servings.

Lime and Tarragon Chicken

quantity	ingredient	carb grams
2 lb.	boneless chicken breasts, cut in 1/2 inch cubes	
2 T.	olive oil	
4 T.	lime juice	4
1/2 c.	dry white wine	1
2 t.	garlic powder	4
1 t.	onion powder	1
1 t.	ginger	1
1/2 t.	tarragon	
1/2 c.	canned chicken stock	1
1/4 c.	tomato sauce	3
	Total Carbohydrate Grams	15
	Carbohydrate Grams per serving	3.8

Method of Preparation:

Marinate the chicken in the seasonings, the lime juice and the wine for at least an hour if possible. Fry the chicken in the oil over medium high heat about 10 minutes. Add the remaining ingredients, cover and bring to a boil. Reduce heat and let simmer 45 minutes. Let sit 5 minutes before serving.

Makes 4 servings.

Chicken with Tarragon Sauce

quantity	ingredient	carb grams
2 lb.	boneless chicken breasts, cut into 1/2 inch cubes	
2 T.	olive oil	
1/2 c.	dry white wine	1
1 T.	Dijon mustard	
2 t.	tarragon	1
1	bouillon cube	1
1/4 c.	heavy cream	2
1/2 t.	black pepper	
	Total Carbohydrate Grams	5
	Carbohydrate Grams per serving	1.3

Method of Preparation:

Fry the chicken in the oil over medium high heat until it begins to brown slightly. Add the wine, pepper and bouillon cube, cover and bring to a boil. Reduce heat and let simmer 20 minutes. Stir in the cream and tarragon and let simmer about 10 minutes until the mixture begins to thicken.

Makes 4 servings.

Korean Bar-B-Q Chicken

quantity	ingredient	carb grams
1	Fryer, cut into pieces (about 3 lbs.)	
1/2 c.	soy sauce	
2 T.	sesame oil	
1 t.	sesame seeds	1
3 T.	sugar equivalent sweetener	
1	bunch scallions, diced	4
1/4 t.	black pepper	
1/2 t.	cayenne pepper	
1 t.	ginger	1
1 t.	garlic powder	2
	Total Carbohydrate Grams	8
	Carbohydrate Grams per serving	2.7

Method of Preparation:

Mix all ingredients. Let marinate 1 hour. Cook over charcoal, basting with the remaining liquid. Serve with Yaki Mandu sauce (p. 233) for dipping.

Makes 3 servings.

Hungarian Chicken Paprika

quantity	ingredient	carb grams
2 lb.	boneless chicken, cut into 1/2 inch cubes	
2 T.	olive oil	
3 T.	paprika	9
2 t.	garlic powder	4
1/2 t.	black pepper	
1/2	medium onion, diced	8
1/2 c.	canned chicken stock	
1 c.	sour cream	6
	Total Carbohydrate Grams	27
	Carbohydrate Grams per serving	6.8

Method of Preparation:

Fry the chicken in the oil over medium high heat until the chicken turns white. Add the onions and cook until they become clear. Add the remaining ingredients except the sour cream, cover and bring to a boil. Reduce heat and simmer 45 minutes. Stir in the sour cream and let sit 5 minutes before serving.

Makes 4 servings.

Seafood Recipes

Crab Stuffed Mushrooms

suggested by Kathy Dempsey

quantity	ingredient	carb grams
12	large fresh mushrooms	
1 c.	crushed pork rinds	
1/4 c.	onion, diced	4
1/4 c.	crabmeat (cooked)	
2 T.	mayonnaise	
1/4 c.	cheeses (i.e. sharp cheddar)	2
2 T.	butter	
	Total Carbohydrate Grams	6
	Carbohydrate Grams per serving	0.5

Method of Preparation:

Remove stems from mushrooms and mince. Sauté onion in butter over medium heat until onions become clear. Remove from heat and sprinkle the cheese over the top, cover with a lid and set aside. After it has cooled to room temperature, mix the onion mixture with the crushed pork rinds, and then add the mayonnaise and crab. Stuff the mushrooms with the mixture and bake in a 375 degree oven about 20 minutes or until they are brown on top.

For variations you can use anything low carb in place of crab, i.e., spinach, broccoli, shrimp, etc.

Makes 12 servings.

Scallops and Crab Alfredo
suggested by Kathy Dempsey

quantity	ingredient	carb grams
1/4 lb.	crabmeat (uncooked)	
1/4 lb.	scallops	
1/2 c.	heavy cream	3
1/2 c.	shredded mozzarella cheese	2
3 T.	Parmesan cheese	1
2 T.	butter	
1/8 t.	salt	
	Total Carbohydrate Grams	6
	Carbohydrate Grams per serving	6

Method of Preparation:

Sauté the crab and scallops in butter over medium high heat until mostly cooked. Add the heavy cream and salt and reduce to medium heat. Add the Parmesan and stir. Add most of the mozzarella and stir until it thickens. Remove to a casserole dish and add the rest of the mozzarella and broil in a toaster oven or regular oven until brown and bubbly on top.

Makes 1 serving.

Southwestern Crabcakes

quantity	ingredient	carb grams
1 lb.	Crabmeat, cooked	
2 t.	garlic powder	4
1/2	medium onion, diced	8
2 t.	dried parsley	
1	stalk celery, diced	2
1/2	medium bell pepper, diced	3
2 T.	pickled jalapeño peppers, diced	1
1/4 c.	mayonnaise	
4 T.	olive oil	
2 t.	Worcestershire Sauce (p. 222)	
1/2 t.	hot pepper sauce (optional)	
1 t.	salt	
1/2 t.	black pepper	
	Total Carbohydrate Grams	18
	Carbohydrate Grams per serving	9.0

Method of Preparation:

Fry the onion, celery and bell pepper over medium heat in 2 T. of olive oil until the onions begin to clear. Remove from the heat and let cool to room temperature. Blend all ingredients. Mold into four patties and fry in 2 T. olive oil until brown on both sides. Serve with Green Chili and Lime Sauce.

Makes 2 servings.

Shrimp Mousse
suggested by Peggy Veitch

quantity	ingredient	carb grams
1 c.	mayonnaise	
6 oz.	cream cheese at room temperature	4
2	cans (6 oz.) canned salad shrimp drained	
1 c.	celery, diced finely	5
1/2 c.	Pickled Onions (p. 216)	8
1 c.	tomato juice	10
1 pack	knox gelatin	
	Total Carbohydrate Grams	27
	Carbohydrate Grams per serving of 1 oz.	0.9

Method of Preparation:

Mix the gelatin with the tomato juice and bring to a boil. Let cool to room temperature. Combine the mayonnaise and cream cheese. Add in the shrimp, celery and onions. Finally add all of this to the tomato juice. Pour into mayonnaise greased pre-cooled mold (or individual containers). Refrigerate 2 hours.

Makes about 4 cups.

Steamed Mussels

suggested by Sarah Armstrong Joyal

quantity	ingredient	carb grams
2 dozen	mussels	
2 oz.	Irish whiskey	
1 bottle	clam juice (about 8 oz.)	
2 T.	butter	
1 T.	tarragon	2
1/2 c.	heavy cream	3
1/2 t.	salt	
1/4 t.	black pepper	
	Total Carbohydrate Grams	5
	Carbohydrate Grams per serving	2.5

Method of Preparation:

Store and clean the mussels as directed by your vendor. Place the mussels in a pan for steaming. Add the whiskey and the clam juice and bring to a boil. Reduce heat and simmer until the mussels are cooked, about 15 minutes. Add the remaining ingredients to the pan and let simmer 10 minutes.

Makes 2 servings.

Hint – One pint of water is equivalent to 16 ounces.

Salmon Loaf

quantity	ingredient	carb grams
1	can (15 oz.) salmon	
1/4 c.	half and half	2
2	eggs, beaten	1
1 t.	salt	
1/4 t.	black pepper	
1 t.	paprika	1
2 t.	Worcestershire Sauce (p. 222)	
2	stalks celery, diced	3
1/4	medium onion, diced	4
2 t.	dried parsley	
2 T.	lemon juice	2
	Total Carbohydrate Grams	13
	Carbohydrate Grams per serving	4.3

Method of Preparation:

Combine all ingredients and mix thoroughly. Pour into an oiled loaf pan. Bake at 350 degrees about 1 hour or until a knife inserted into the center comes out clean.

Makes 3 servings.

Shrimp Szechwan

quantity	ingredient	carb grams
1 lb.	uncooked shrimp	
1 t.	garlic powder	2
1 t.	ginger	1
2 t.	dried red pepper flakes	1
2 T.	soy sauce	
2 T.	Ketchup (p. 219)	2
1	bunch scallions, sliced	4
2 t.	sugar equivalent sweetener	
2 T.	peanut oil	
2 t.	sesame oil	
2 T.	water	
	Total Carbohydrate Grams	10
	Carbohydrate Grams per serving	5.0

Method of Preparation:

Heat the peanut oil over high heat. Cook the shrimp quickly over the high heat until they turn white. Add the water and soy sauce and bring to a boil. Add the remaining ingredients except the onion and simmer about 5 minutes stirring to ensure that the shrimp are coated. Add the onion and simmer another 2 minutes. A variation on this is to use diced chicken rather than shrimp but it must be cooked longer, 20 minutes if the pieces are small, up to 45 minutes if you cut the chicken in 1/2-inch cubes.

Makes 2 servings.

Shrimp Remoulade

quantity	ingredient	carb grams
1 lb.	peeled shrimp	
1/2 lb.	scallops	
1/2 lb.	smoked polish sausage, diced	8
2 T.	olive oil	
1 t.	garlic powder	2
1 t.	onion powder	1
1 t.	thyme	1
1 t.	cayenne pepper	1
1 t.	salt	
1/2 t.	black pepper	
1/2 c.	Remoulade Sauce (p. 237)	3
1/2 c.	heavy cream	3
1/4 c	water	
	Total Carbohydrate Grams	19
	Carbohydrate Grams per serving	4.8

Method of Preparation:

Fry the sausage in the oil over medium high heat about 2 minutes. Add the shrimp, scallops and seasonings and cook until the shrimp turn white. Add the water and bring to a boil. Add the remoulade sauce and cream and reduce for about 5 minutes. Let sit about 5 minutes before serving.

Makes 4 servings.

Shrimp Jambalaya

quantity	ingredient	carb grams
2 lb.	peeled shrimp	
1/2 lb.	boneless cooked chicken, cubed	
1/2 lb.	smoked polish sausage, cubed	8
3 T.	olive oil	
1	medium onion, sliced	16
1	medium bell pepper, sliced	6
4	stalks celery, sliced	6
1	bunch scallions, sliced	4
2 t.	garlic powder	4
1 t.	thyme	1
1 t.	cayenne pepper	1
1/2 t.	black pepper	
1/2 t.	salt	
2 T.	Worcestershire Sauce (p. 222)	
1/2 c.	canned chicken stock	
1/2 c.	tomato sauce	6
	Total Carbohydrate Grams	52
	Carbohydrate Grams per serving	8.7

Method of Preparation:

Fry the sausage and chicken in the oil over medium high heat until they begin cooking, that is, they aren't just heated up. Add the onions, celery, bell pepper, and scallions and cook until the onions become clear. Add the shrimp and the dry seasonings and cook until the shrimp begin to turn white. Add the remaining ingredients, bring to a boil and simmer about 5 minutes.

Makes 6 servings.

Main Courses - Other

One Pan Pizza Casserole

quantity	ingredient	carb grams
1/2 lb.	Italian Sausage (p. 139)	
1/2 lb.	sliced pepperoni	
1/2	medium onion, diced	8
1	medium bell pepper, diced	6
1 c.	mushroom, diced	4
1/4 c.	dry red wine	1
1 t.	Italian seasoning	1
1/4 c.	Ketchup (p. 219)	3
1/2 lb.	shredded mozzarella cheese	4
1/4 c.	Parmesan cheese	2
	Total Carbohydrate Grams	30
	Carbohydrate Grams per serving	10.0

Method of Preparation:

In an ovenproof skillet, fry the Italian sausage over medium heat until it is cooked thoroughly, breaking it into small pieces. Add the onion and cook until they become clear. Add the bell pepper and mushrooms and cook until the mushrooms begin to wilt. Add the seasonings, pepperoni, wine and ketchup and let reduce uncovered 5 minutes. Turn on the broiler in your oven. Sprinkle the Parmesan cheese over the contents of the pan, then the mozzarella. Place under the broiler until the cheese is lightly browned.

Makes 3 servings.

Basic Breakfast Sausage

There have been several complaints about trying to find a commercial breakfast sausage which doesn't have any carbs. Now you can make your own.

quantity	ingredient	carb grams
1 lb.	lean ground pork	
1 t.	salt	
1/2 t.	black pepper	
1/4 t.	cayenne pepper	
1/2 t.	sage	
1 t.	garlic powder (optional)	
	Total Carbohydrate Grams	
	Carbohydrate Grams per serving	0

Method of Preparation:

Mix all ingredients. Let sit refrigerated for a couple of hours if possible. Separate into 4 patties and cook over medium to low heat until they are well done.

Makes 4 servings.

Hint – One quart of water is equivalent to 32 ounces.

Bratwurst Recipe (1)

quantity	ingredient	carb grams
5 lb.	lean ground pork	
1	egg beaten	
1 c.	dry German white wine	1
1 t.	black pepper	
2 T.	salt	
2 t.	mace	2
2 t.	nutmeg	2
1 t.	ginger	1
1 t.	mustard seed	1
2 T.	garlic powder	12
1 T.	onion powder	3
	Total Carbohydrate Grams	22
	Carbohydrate Grams per serving	1.1

Method of Preparation:

Mix dry ingredients and liquids. Then add the meat and blend well. Let sit at least 10 minutes before cooking, overnight is better. Patty out to 4 oz. servings. If freezing, ensure the package to be as airtight as possible in order to prevent freezer burn.

Makes about 20 servings.

Bratwurst Recipe (2)

quantity	ingredient	carb grams
3 lb.	lean ground pork	
3 lb.	lean ground veal	
1 1/2c.	dry German white wine	1
1 t.	white pepper	1
2 T.	salt	
2 t.	mace	2
2 t.	nutmeg	2
2 T.	garlic powder	12
1 T.	onion powder	3
	Total Carbohydrate Grams	21
	Carbohydrate Grams per serving	0.8

Method of Preparation:

Mix dry ingredients and liquids. Then add the meat and blend well. Let sit at least 10 minutes before cooking, overnight is better. Patty out to 4 oz. servings. If freezing, ensure the package to be as airtight as possible in order to prevent freezer burn.

Makes about 24 servings.

Hint – One quart is equivalent to two pints.

Bratwurst Recipe (3)

quantity	ingredient	carb grams
3 lb.	lean ground pork	
1/2 c.	dry German white wine	1
1/2 t.	white pepper	
1 T.	salt	
1/4 t.	allspice	
1/2 t.	caraway	
1/2 t.	marjoram	1
2 t.	garlic powder	4
1 t.	onion powder	1
	Total Carbohydrate Grams	7
	Carbohydrate Grams per serving	0.6

Method of Preparation:

Mix dry ingredients and liquids. Then add the meat and blend well. Let sit at least 10 minutes before cooking, overnight is better. Patty out to 4 oz. servings. If freezing, ensure the package to be as airtight as possible in order to prevent freezer burn.

Makes about 12 servings.

Bratwurst Recipe (4)

Bratwurst Wisconsin Style

quantity	ingredient	carb grams
4 lb.	lean ground pork	
2 lb.	lean ground turkey	
1/2 c.	dry German white wine	1
1/2 c.	half and half	8
2	eggs beaten	1
1 t.	white pepper	1
2 T.	salt	
1/4 t.	ground cloves	
1/4 t.	nutmeg	1
1 t.	mustard seed	1
2 T.	garlic powder	12
1 T.	onion powder	3
	Total Carbohydrate Grams	28
	Carbohydrate Grams per serving	1.2

Method of Preparation:

Mix dry ingredients and liquids. Then add the meat and blend well. Let sit at least 10 minutes before cooking, overnight is better. Patty out to 4 oz. servings. If freezing, ensure the package to be as airtight as possible in order to prevent freezer burn.

Makes about 24 servings.

Brats and Beer

quantity	ingredient	carb grams
	enough brats for 2 people	4
1 can	low carb beer	3
1/2	medium onion, sliced	8
3 T.	butter	
2	bouillon cubes	2
	Total Carbohydrate Grams	17
	Carbohydrate Grams per serving	8.5

Method of Preparation (1):

Parboil the brats before cooking. Fry the onions in the butter until they begin to brown slightly. Add the beer and bouillon cubes and bring to a boil. Reduce the heat to low. Drop the brats into the liquid and cook them until they are gray. The object is to keep them at a temperature of about 180 degrees for about 15 minutes. After you have parboiled the brats, you can cook them slowly, either in a skillet or on the grill. When they are finished cooking, place them into the broth and keep them there at about 160 degrees for 20 or 30 minutes (or longer). Serve with some of the onions and broth.

Method of Preparation (2):

Prepare the onions and beer as described in method 1 above. If you are using commercially prepared brats in casings, slice the bratwurst in half lengthwise, but not all the way through and flatten them before putting them on the hot grill. If you are using brats that you made yourself, this is not a problem. Turning only once, cook the brats until they are nicely browned on both sides. Add the grilled bratwursts to the beer and keep warm until ready to serve. These are especially good when they are allowed to sit overnight in the beer and then reheated the next day. Serve with plenty of mustard and warmed sauerkraut.

Makes 2 servings.

Curried Bratwurst

quantity	ingredient	carb grams
4 lb.	ground pork	
4 t.	salt	
1 c.	water	
2 t.	curry powder	2
2 t.	coriander	1
2 t.	white pepper	
1 t.	dry mustard	1
1 t.	ginger	1
	Total Carbohydrate Grams	5
	Carbohydrate Grams per serving	0.3

Method of Preparation:

Mix all ingredients thoroughly.

Makes 16 servings.

Ukrainian Kielbasa

quantity	ingredient	carb grams
5 lb.	ground pork	
1 lb.	ground beef	
1 ib.	ground turkey	
2 T.	salt	
1 T.	garlic powder	6
1 T.	mustard seed	3
1 c.	water	
1 T.	paprika	3
	Total Carbohydrate Grams	12
	Carbohydrate Grams per serving	0.4

Method of Preparation:

Mix all ingredients. Let sit refrigerated overnight if possible.

Makes 28 servings.

Lithuanian Kielbasa

quantity	ingredient	carb grams
5 lb.	ground pork	
2 t.	dry mustard	2
2 t.	allspice	2
1/2 t.	black pepper	
5 t.	salt	
2 T.	garlic powder	6
1 T.	onion powder	3
1 c.	water	
	Total Carbohydrate Grams	19
	Carbohydrate Grams per serving	1.0

Method of Preparation:

Mix all ingredients thoroughly. Let sit refrigerated overnight if possible.

Makes 20 servings.

Kielbasa and White Wine

quantity	ingredient	carb grams
1 lb.	any Kielbasa (pp. 132-133)	2
1 T.	olive oil	
1/2 c.	dry white wine	1
2 t.	sugar equivalent sweetener	
1 T.	Dijon mustard	
1 t.	dried parsley	
1/4 t.	black pepper	
	Total Carbohydrate Grams	3
	Carbohydrate Grams per serving	1.5

Method of Preparation:

Make 4 patties, 4 oz. each. Fry the sausage in the oil over medium high heat until it is browned on each side. Add the remaining ingredients, cover and bring to a boil. Reduce heat and simmer 15 minutes. Remove the lid and let simmer an additional 5 minutes.

Makes 2 servings.

Kielbasa with Chili Sauce

quantity	ingredient	carb grams
1 lb.	any Kielbasa (pp. 132-133)	2
1 T.	olive oil	
1/2 c.	Chili Sauce (p. 220)	5
1/4 c.	sugar equivalent sweetener	
1/2 c.	canned chicken broth	
	Total Carbohydrate Grams	7
	Carbohydrate Grams per serving	0.4

Method of Preparation:

Make the kielbase into 1oz. meat balls. Fry over medium heat until browned on both sides. Add remaining ingredients, cover and bring to a boil. Let simmer 20 minutes. Serve as appetizers.

Makes 16 servings.

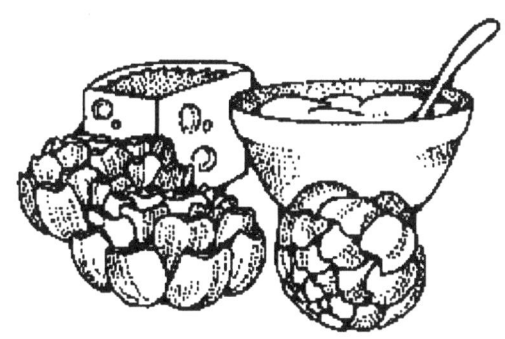

Polish Sausage

quantity	ingredient	carb grams
5 lb.	ground pork	
1/2 pt.	half and half	8
5 t.	salt	
2 T.	sugar equivalent sweetener	
1 T.	black pepper	
1 T.	coriander	1
2 T.	garlic powder	12
1 T.	onion powder	6
	Total Carbohydrate Grams	21
	Carbohydrate Grams per serving	1.1

Method of Preparation:

Dissolve the sweetener in the half and half. Mix all ingredients thoroughly. Let sit refrigerated overnight if possible.

Makes 20 servings.

Polish Kielbasa and Cabbage

quantity	ingredient	carb grams
4 oz.	butter	
1/2	medium onion, sliced	8
2 lb.	cabbage cut into 2 inch cubes	40
2 lb.	smoked polish sausage, sliced in 1/4 inch pieces	32
2 T.	sugar equivalent sweetener	
1 t.	salt	
1/2 t.	black pepper	
1/2 c.	canned beef stock	
	Total Carbohydrate Grams	80
	Carbohydrate Grams per serving	20.0

Method of Preparation:

Cook the onion in the butter over medium heat until the onion is clear. Add the cabbage, beef stock, sweetener, salt and pepper, cover and bring to a boil. Reduce heat and simmer about 30 minutes until the cabbage is tender. Add the sausage and let simmer uncovered about 5 minutes.

Makes 4 servings.

Polish Sausage in Red Wine

quantity	ingredient	carb grams
1 lb.	Polish Sausage (p 136)	2
2 T.	olive oil	
1/4	medium onion, diced	4
1	bunch scallions, sliced	4
1 c.	dry red wine	1
1	bouillon cube	1
	Total Carbohydrate Grams	12
	Carbohydrate Grams per serving	6.0

Method of Preparation:

Form the polish sausage into 4 oz. patties. Cook the sausage in the oil over medium high heat until it is browned on both sides. Turn only once. Remove the meat to a plate, reserving the oil. Cook the onions and scallions until the onions become clear. Return the meat to the skillet and add the remaining ingredients. Cover and bring to a boil. Reduce heat and simmer 20 minutes.

Makes 2 servings.

Italian Sausage

Italian sausage is especially good when grilled.

quantity	ingredient	carb grams
3 lb.	ground pork	
1 c.	dry red wine	1
1 T.	salt	
1 T.	sugar equivalent sweetener	
1 t.	black pepper	
1 T.	fennel or anise seed	3
2 t.	coriander	1
2 t.	cayenne	2
1 T.	Italian seasoning	2
1 T.	garlic powder	6
2 t.	onion powder	2
1 T.	dried parsley	
2 T.	paprika	5
2 T.	Serbian Peppers (optional)	
1 t.	caraway seed (optional)	
	Total Carbohydrate Grams	22
	Carbohydrate Grams per serving	1.8

Method of Preparation:

Mix all ingredients thoroughly. Let sit refrigerated overnight if possible.

Makes 12 servings.

Italian Sausage and Peppers

quantity	ingredient	carb grams
1 lb.	Italian Sausage (p. 139)	7
1/2	medium onion, sliced	8
2	medium bell peppers, sliced	12
4 T.	olive oil	
1/2 c.	canned beef broth	
1/2 c.	Ketchup (p. 219)	6
1/2 t.	Italian seasoning	
	Total Carbohydrate Grams	33
	Carbohydrate Grams per serving	16.5

Method of Preparation:

Form the sausage into 4 oz. patties. Fry the onion in 2 T. oil over medium heat until it begins to clear. Set aside. Add the remaining oil to the skillet and fry the sausage, browning on both sides. Add all ingredients, cover and bring to a boil. Reduce the heat and simmer 15 minutes. Let sit 5 minutes before serving.

Makes 2 servings.

Creole Hot Sausage

quantity	ingredient	carb grams
4 lb.	ground pork	
2 t.	garlic powder	4
4 t.	salt	
4 t.	paprika	4
2 t.	onion powder	2
2 t.	Italian seasoning	1
2 t.	cayenne pepper	2
2 t.	black pepper	
1 c.	water	
2 t.	sugar equivalent sweetener	
	Total Carbohydrate Grams	13
	Carbohydrate Grams per serving	0.8

Method of Preparation:

Mix all ingredients thoroughly. Let sit refrigerated overnight if possible.

Makes 16 servings.

Jambalaya

quantity	ingredient	carb grams
1 lb.	boneless chicken, cut in 1/2 inch cubes	
1/2 lb.	baked ham, cut in 1/2 inch cubes	
1/2 lb.	polish kielbasa, cut in 1/2 inch cubes	8
2 T.	olive oil	
1/2	medium onion, sliced	8
1	medium bell pepper, sliced	6
1	bunch scallions, sliced	4
1/2	medium carrot, diced	4
2	stalks celery, diced	3
2 t.	garlic powder	4
1 T.	dried parsley	
1 t.	salt	
1/2 t.	black pepper	
1/2 t.	cayenne pepper	
2 t.	pickled jalapeño peppers	1
1 t.	ground cumin	1
2	bay leaves	
1/2 t.	cloves	
1/4 t.	thyme	
1/4 t.	basil	
1/4 t.	mace	
1 c.	water	
1 c.	tomato sauce	12
	Total Carbohydrate Grams	51
	Carbohydrate Grams per serving	12.8

Jambalaya

Method of Preparation:

Fry the chicken in the oil over medium high heat until it begins to brown slightly. Add the onion, carrot and celery and cook until the onion becomes clear. Add the other meats and cook until they begin cooking themselves (rather than just being heated up). Add all remaining ingredients, cover and bring to a boil. Let simmer 45 minutes.

Makes 4 servings.

Cajun Chorizo

quantity	ingredient	carb grams
4 lb.	ground pork	
2 t.	onion powder	2
2 t.	garlic powder	4
1 T.	red pepper flakes	1
1 T.	chili powder	3
4 t.	salt	
2 t.	thyme	
1 T.	dried parsley	
1 t.	allspice	1
1 c.	water	
	Total Carbohydrate Grams	11
	Carbohydrate Grams per serving	0.7

Method of Preparation:

Mix all ingredients thoroughly.

Makes 16 servings.

English Bangers

quantity	ingredient	carb grams
4 lb.	ground pork	
1 c.	water	
2 t.	white pepper	
1 t.	mace	1
4 t.	salt	
1 t.	ginger	1
1 t.	sage	
1 t.	nutmeg	1
	Total Carbohydrate Grams	3
	Carbohydrate Grams per serving	0.2

Method of Preparation:

Mix all ingredients thoroughly. Let sit refrigerated overnight if possible.

Makes 16 servings.

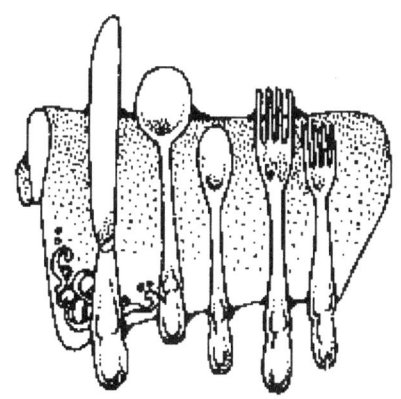

Mexican Chorizo

Chorizo is especially good with eggs.

quantity	ingredient	carb grams
1 lb.	ground pork	
1 t.	salt	
2 T.	chili powder	6
1/2 t.	oregano	
1 t.	garlic powder	2
1/2 t.	onion powder	
2 T.	vinegar	
1/2 c.	water	
	Total Carbohydrate Grams	8
	Carbohydrate Grams per serving	2.0

Method of Preparation:

Mix all ingredients thoroughly. Let sit refrigerated overnight if possible.

Makes 4 servings.

Hungarian Kolbasz

quantity	ingredient	carb grams
4 lb.	ground pork	
3 T.	paprika	9
4 t.	salt	
1 c.	water	
1 T.	ground allspice	2
2 t.	garlic powder	4
1 t.	onion powder	1
	Total Carbohydrate Grams	16
	Carbohydrate Grams per serving	1.0

Method of Preparation:

Mix all ingredients thoroughly. Let sit refrigerated overnight if possible. Traditionally, these sausages are parboiled and served with sour cream and horseradish.

Makes 16 servings.

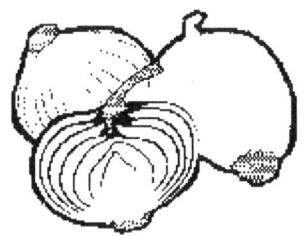

Beef Salami
(no nitrates or nitrates)

quantity	ingredient	carb grams
1 lb.	hamburger (70% lean)	
2 t.	salt	
2 t.	liquid smoke	
1 t.	garlic powder	2
1/2 t.	black pepper	
2 t.	mustard seed	2
1 t.	sugar equivalent sweetener	
2 T.	water	
	Total Carbohydrate Grams	4
	Carbohydrate Grams per serving	0.3

Method of Preparation:

Mix everything except the hamburger in a microwavable bowl. Microwave 20-30 seconds, until it almost boils.   Let cool to room temperature. Mix everything together very thoroughly, place in a bowl, cover and refrigerate 24 - 48 hours. Form in a roll, place on a rack on a baking sheet, and cook at 240 degrees for 2 1/2 hours. After it is cooked, place on a plate and let cool to room temperature. Wrap tightly in a plastic bag and refrigerate.

Makes 16 servings.

German Mortadella
(no nitrates or nitrites)

quantity	ingredient	carb grams
2 lb.	ground pork	
4 t.	salt	
1 T.	liquid smoke	
1 T.	garlic powder	6
2 t.	onion powder	2
1 t.	white pepper	
1 T.	sugar equivalent sweetener	
4 T.	water	
1 t.	cardamom	1
2 t.	coriander	1
1 t.	clove	1
2 t.	rum (very optional)	
1 t.	dill	
1 t.	caraway	1
1 oz.	pistachio nuts (optional)	8
1 T.	vinegar	
	Total Carbohydrate Grams	20
	Carbohydrate Grams per serving	0.6

Method of Preparation:

Mix everything except the pork and pistachio nuts in a microwavable bowl. Microwave 30 seconds, until it almost boils. Let cool to room temperature. Mix everything thoroughly, place in a bowl, cover and refrigerate 24 - 48 hours. Form in two rolls, place on a rack on a baking sheet and cook at 240 degrees for 3 hours. After they are cooked, place on a plate and let cool to room temperature. Wrap tightly in plastic bags and refrigerate.

Makes 32 servings.

Schlacht Platte (German)

The Schlacht Platte is a sausage sampler with other foods attached. For Germans, this other food normally includes a vegetable, potato salad, bread and beer. We can still have a Schlacht Platte but only with our low carb vegetables. A good example of this would be to take, per person, any three or four of the following types of sausages (among others):

> Beef Salami
> Mortadella
> Bratwurst
> Knackwurst
> Polish Sausage
> Ukrainian Kielbase

Cook these sausages in whatever manner you choose for that day; you can fry, broil, boil, or Bar-B-Q them. Serve them with (again, among others):

> Sauerkraut (p.189)
> Red Cabbage (pp. 184-186)
> Cucumber-Zucchini salad (p. 30)
> Hot Cauliflower Salad (p. 183)
> Various other salads/vegetables which involve vinegar and oil
> Green Beans (p. 181)

If you can afford a couple of low carb beers within your carb limit, then go for the gusto.

Gnaedigen Damen und Herren, Guten Appetit!!

Italian Meatballs

quantity	ingredient	carb grams
3 lb.	lean ground beef	
1/2	medium onion, diced	8
2 t.	garlic powder	4
1 T.	dried parsley	
1	Egg, beaten slightly	1
1/2 c.	water	
2 T.	olive oil	
1 T.	salt	
1/2 t.	black pepper	
1/2 t.	nutmeg	
	Total Carbohydrate Grams	13
	Carbohydrate Grams per serving	0.5

Method of Preparation:

Mix all ingredients thoroughly. Let sit 10 minutes. Form into 2 oz. balls. Fry in the oil over medium heat until browned all over.

Makes 24 servings.

It seems that everyone now has a recipe for chicken wings. They have become a staple in our cuisine. If I really wanted to become wealthy, I would develop a chicken with four wings. You can get Buffalo wings, Syracuse wings, Montreal wings, Texas wings, Cajun wings, Korean wings and River City wings. It also seems that everyone has their own way to prepare the "original" recipe or Buffalo wings from the Anchor Bar in Buffalo. One person says you should use only margarine. Another person says that you should use only a certain type of hot sauce. Another person claims that the Bleu Cheese dressing is a dip for the wings and not the celery and another says that the proper ratio of hot pepper sauce to oil is 3:1. Whatever the case, wings are especially good for low carb eaters. Herewith are about a dozen and a half recipes, beginning with the simplest.

Buffalo Wings (1)
(a simpler recipe)

quantity	ingredient	carb grams
2 lb.	chicken wings	
1 T.	butter or margarine	
1/4 c.	hot pepper sauce	4
1 t.	salt	
	Total Carbohydrate Grams	4
	Carbohydrate Grams per serving	2.0

Method of Preparation:

Melt the butter in a sauce pan. Add the hot sauce and the salt. Fry the wings in 375 degree oil until they are brown and crisp. Place the wings in a bowl that can be covered. Add the sauce and shake well insuring that they are evenly coated. Serve with Bleu Cheese dressing (p. 17) and celery sticks.

Makes about 2 servings.

Buffalo Wings (2)

quantity	ingredient	carb grams
2 lb.	chicken wings	
1/2	stick butter or margarine	
1 T.	white vinegar	
1 oz.	hot pepper sauce	2
1 t.	salt	
1/8 t.	celery seed	
1/4 t.	cayenne pepper	
1 t.	garlic powder	2
1/2 t.	black pepper	
	Total Carbohydrate Grams	4
	Carbohydrate Grams per serving	2.0

Method of Preparation:

Melt the butter in a sauce pan. Add the hot sauce, vinegar, the spices and the salt. Cook until the sauce thickens slightly. Fry the wings in 375 degree oil until they are brown and crisp. Place the wings in a bowl that can be covered. Add the sauce and shake well insuring that they are evenly coated. After they are coated they can be baked for 10 to 15 minutes at 375 degrees to "dry up" the sauce. Serve with Bleu Cheese dressing (p. 17) and celery sticks.

Makes about 2 servings.

Garlic Wings

Chicken Wings and Garlic. Just add a six pack of low carb beer and you have the eight major food groups.

quantity	ingredient	carb grams
2 lbs.	wings, separated	
1/2 c.	olive oil	
2 oz.	cloves garlic, whole and peeled	18
1/2 t.	rosemary	
1/2 t.	thyme	
1 t.	onion powder	
2 t.	dry white wine	
1 t.	salt	
	Total Carbohydrate Grams	18
	Carbohydrate Grams per serving	9.0

Method of Preparation:

Heat oven to 375 degrees. Place all ingredients in casserole, tossing to coat evenly. Cover and bake one hour stirring a couple of times. Serve with the olive oil as a dip. The garlic can be eaten with a fork.

Makes about 2 servings.

Mexican Wings Verde

quantity	ingredient	carb grams
2 lb.	chicken wings, separated	
1 c.	water	
1/2	medium onion, diced	8
2	bouillon cubes	2
1 t.	garlic powder	2
3 T.	pickled jalapeño peppers	2
	Total Carbohydrate Grams	14
	Carbohydrate Grams per serving	6.7

Method of Preparation:

Put all ingredients in a pan, cover and bring to a boil. Stir, reduce heat and simmer 30 - 45 minutes, stirring every 10 minutes until the meat is falling away from the bones. Serve some of the stock as a dip.

Makes about 2 servings.

Hint – One cup of water is equivalent to eight ounces.

Bar-B-Q Wings

quantity	ingredient	carb grams
2 lb.	chicken wings, separated	
1c.	basic Bar-B-Q sauce (p. 224)	12
	Total Carbohydrate Grams	12
	Carbohydrate Grams per serving	6.0

Method of Preparation:

Place all ingredients in a sauce pan, cover and bring to a boil. Reduce heat and let simmer about 15 minutes. Remove wings to a baking sheet (single layer) and bake at 375 degrees for 30 minutes. Increase heat to 425 degrees and begin basting with the remaining sauce, cooking an additional 15 minutes. Serve with the remaining sauce.

Makes about 2 servings.

Baked Buffalo Wings

quantity	ingredient	carb grams
2 lb.	chicken wings	
1	stick butter or margarine	
1/3 c.	hot pepper sauce	4
1/3 c.	white vinegar	
1 t.	salt	
1 t.	garlic powder	2
1 t.	onion powder	1
	Total Carbohydrate Grams	7
	Carbohydrate Grams per serving	3.5

Method of Preparation:

Melt the butter in a sauce pan. Add the hot sauce, vinegar, spices and the salt and bring to a boil. Bake the wings in a 375 degree oven until they are done, about 30 - 40 minutes. Place the wings in a bowl which can be covered. Add the sauce and shake well insuring that they are evenly coated. Serve with Bleu Cheese dressing (p. 17) and celery sticks.

Makes about 2 servings.

Cajun Bar-B-Q Wings

quantity	ingredient	carb grams
2 lb.	chicken wings, separated	
3 T.	red pepper sauce	3
3 T.	Cajun Seasoning (p. 231)	9
2 T.	cooking oil	
	Total Carbohydrate Grams	12
	Carbohydrate Grams per serving	6.0

Method of Preparation:

In a small bow, mix the pepper sauce, Cajun seasoning and cooking oil. Place the wings in a larger bowl. Pour the seasoning sauce over the wings and mix well. Cook these slowly on the Bar-B-Q grill, basting with any remaining sauce. Serve with red pepper sauce if desired.

Makes about 2 servings.

Kansas City Style Wings

quantity	ingredient	carb grams
3 lb.	Wings, split	
1/2 c.	Dijon mustard	
2 t.	olive oil	
2 t.	garlic powder	4
1/2 c.	soy sauce	
1/2 t.	ginger	
1 t.	onion powder	1
	Total Carbohydrate Grams	5
	Carbohydrate Grams per serving	1.7

Method of Preparation:

Mix all ingredients and marinate at least an hour. Grill the wings basting with the sauce. Discard any remaining sauce after the wings are finished cooking.

Makes 3 servings.

Devilled Chicken Wings

quantity	ingredient	carb grams
2 lb.	chicken wings, split	
3 T.	olive oil	
1/2 c.	Chili Sauce (p. 220)	5
1/4 c.	tomato juice	4
1 T.	horseradish	2
1 T.	mustard	
2 t.	Worcestershire Sauce (p. 222)	
1/2 t.	salt	
1 T.	cayenne pepper	3
1 t.	garlic powder	2
1 t.	onion powder	1
2 t.	paprika	2
	Total Carbohydrate Grams	19
	Carbohydrate Grams per serving	9.5

Method of Preparation:

Fry the wings in the oil over medium heat until they begin to brown. Add remaining ingredients, cover and bring to a boil. Reduce heat and simmer 45 minutes.

Makes 2 servings.

Caribbean Wings

quantity	ingredient	carb grams
2 lb.	chicken wings, separated	
4 T.	lime juice	4
1 t.	garlic powder	2
1 t.	onion powder	1
1 t.	paprika	1
1/2 t.	black pepper	
1 T.	soy sauce	
	Total Carbohydrate Grams	8
	Carbohydrate Grams per serving	4.0

Method of Preparation:

Combine all ingredients and marinate for at least an hour. Bake covered at 350 degrees for 30 minutes. Remove cover and bake until liquid is reduced to a syrup.

Makes 2 servings.

Lemon Wings

quantity	ingredient	carb grams
2 lb.	chicken wings, separated	
3 T.	soy sauce	
3 T.	dry white wine	1
3 T.	olive oil	
1/2 c.	canned chicken broth	
2 T.	lemon juice	2
1 T.	lemon zest	1
3 T.	sugar equivalent sweetener	
1 t.	sesame oil	
3 t.	ginger	3
1 t.	garlic powder	2
1 t.	onion powder	1
	Total Carbohydrate Grams	10
	Carbohydrate Grams per serving	5.0

Method of Preparation:

Fry the wings in the olive oil over medium heat until they begin the brown. Add the remaining ingredients, cover, and bring to a boil. Reduce heat and simmer 30 - 45 minutes.

Makes 2 servings.

Parmesan Wings

quantity	ingredient	carb grams
2 lb.	chicken wings separated	
1/2	stick butter	
2 T.	Dijon mustard	
1 T.	lemon juice	1
1 t.	garlic powder	2
1 t.	onion powder	1
1/2 c.	canned chicken stock	
1/2 t.	salt	
1/2 t.	black pepper	
1/2 t.	oregano	
1/2 c.	Parmesan cheese	1
	Total Carbohydrate Grams	5
	Carbohydrate Grams per serving	2.5

Method of Preparation:

Fry the wings in the butter over medium heat until they begin to brown slightly. Add the remaining ingredients except the Parmesan cheese, cover and bring to a boil. Reduce heat and simmer 30 - 45 minutes. Sprinkle the Parmesan cheese in slowly and coat evenly.

Makes 2 servings.

Thai Chicken Wings

quantity	ingredient	carb grams
2 lb.	chicken wings, separated	
3 T.	peanut butter	12
3 t.	curry powder	3
4 T.	Thai fish sauce	
1/2 t.	pepper	
1 t.	garlic powder	2
1 t.	onion powder	1
3 T.	lemon juice	3
3 T.	lime juice	3
3 T.	sugar equivalent sweetener	
4 T.	soy sauce	
2 T.	ginger	6
2 T.	peanut oil	
1 T.	Tabasco sauce	
	Total Carbohydrate Grams	30
	Carbohydrate Grams per serving	15.0

Method of Preparation:

Mix all ingredients except the chicken thoroughly. Add the chicken and marinate at least an hour. Grill the wings until they are done, basting with the remaining marinade.

Makes 2 servings.

Horseradish Wings

quantity	ingredient	carb grams
2 lb.	chicken wings, separated	
1/2 c.	Ketchup (p. 219)	6
4 T.	horseradish	8
3 T.	olive oil	
3 T.	Worcestershire Sauce (p. 222)	
1 t.	Tabasco sauce	
1/2 t.	black pepper	
	Total Carbohydrate Grams	14
	Carbohydrate Grams per serving	7

Method of Preparation:

Marinade all ingredients for at least an hour. Grill until they are cooked, basting with the remaining marinade.

Makes 2 servings.

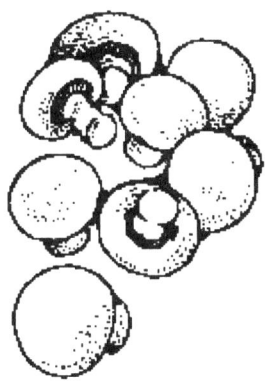

Korean Wings

quantity	ingredient	carb grams
2 lb.	chicken wings separated	
6 T.	Yaki Mandu Sauce (p. 233) for marinade	
	Yaki Mandu Sauce for dipping	
	Total Carbohydrate Grams	
	Carbohydrate Grams per serving	0

Method of Preparation:

Marinate the wings at least an hour. Grill the wings until they are cooked, basting with the marinade. Serve with more Yaki Mandu sauce. Do not consume any of the marinade that isn't used.

Makes 2 servings.

Dragon Breath Wings

quantity	ingredient	carb grams
2 lb.	chicken wings, separated	
1/4 c.	soy sauce	
1 t.	garlic powder	2
1 t.	onion powder	1
1 t.	five spice powder	1
1/4 c.	dry white wine	1
1 T.	sesame oil	
1 t.	Tabasco sauce	
	Total Carbohydrate Grams	5
	Carbohydrate Grams per serving	2.5

Method of Preparation:

Marinate wings overnight. Grill until they are done. Baste with remaining sauce.

Makes 2 servings.

River City "Hawg Wings"

This delicacy was inspired by those "die hard" low fat dieters who will believe that low carb eating plans work and are healthy for the individual "when pigs fly." Unfortunately for the low-fatters, a few of the winged swine have recently been spotted over Iowa. One restaurant entrepreneur in the fabled River City has managed to figure out how to trap these elusive animals and now there is this recipe for River City Wings to go along with all of the other regional variations.

quantity	ingredient	carb grams
2 lb.	boneless pork wing meat cut into 1/2 inch cubes (if you can't yet find pork wings at your local grocery then it is permissible to use pork roast)	
1/2 c.	Chili Sauce (p. 220)	5
2 oz.	red wine ("sour grapes") vinegar	
1/4 c.	soy sauce	
2 t.	red pepper flakes	1
1/2 t.	white pepper	
2 T.	butter	
1/4	medium onion, diced	4
1 t.	garlic powder	2
1 oz.	Tabasco sauce	1
1 oz.	sour mash whiskey (optional)	1
4 T.	sugar equivalent sweetener	
	Total Carbohydrate Grams	14
	Carbohydrate Grams per serving	3.5

Method of Preparation:

Cook your pork wing meat in the butter over medium high heat until it begins to brown slightly. Add the onion and cook until it becomes clear. Add the remaining ingredients, cover and bring to a boil. Reduce heat and simmer 45 minutes. Let sit 5 minutes before serving.

Makes 4 servings.

Cuban Chicken Gizzards

quantity	ingredient	carb grams
1 lb.	chicken gizzards	
1/4	medium onion, sliced	4
1	medium bell pepper, diced	6
1 t.	Tabasco sauce	
1/2 t.	salt	
1/2 t.	black pepper	
1 t	garlic powder	2
2 T.	olive oil	
1/8 c.	water	
2 T.	Faux Balsamic Vinegar (p. 223)	
1/4 c.	Chili Sauce (p. 220)	3
	Total Carbohydrate Grams	15
	Carbohydrate Grams per serving	7.5

Method of Preparation:

Fry the gizzards in the oil until they are all beginning to whiten. Add the onion and cook until the onion becomes clear. Add the remaining ingredients, cover and bring to a boil. Reduce heat and let simmer 20 minutes.

Makes 2 servings.

Chopped Chicken Liver

quantity	ingredient	carb grams
1 lb.	chicken livers	15
1/2	medium onion, diced	8
1/8 c.	water	
2 T.	olive oil	
1 t.	salt	
1/2 t.	black pepper	
2 T.	chicken fat or mayonnaise	
2	hard boiled eggs	1
	Total Carbohydrate Grams	24
	Carbohydrate Grams per serving of 1 T.	1.6

Method of Preparation:

Fry the onion in the olive oil over medium high heat until the onions become clear. Add the water, salt and livers, cover and bring to a boil. Reduce heat and let simmer 30 minutes. Remove the lid and continue cook until the liquid evaporates. Continue cooking about 5 minutes. Remove from the heat and let cool to room temperature. Refrigerate overnight. The next day, mix the liver and eggs in a food processor. The final step is to mix in the chicken fat or mayonnaise.

Makes about 1 pound.

Veal Marsala

quantity	ingredient	carb grams
4	veal cutlets	
1/4 c.	marsala wine	8
1/4 c.	canned beef stock	
1 c.	sliced mushrooms	4
4 T.	butter	
1 t.	garlic powder	2
1/4	medium onion, diced	4
1/2 t.	pepper	
	Total Carbohydrate Grams	18
	Carbohydrate Grams per serving	9.0

Method of Preparation:

Fry cutlets in 2 T. butter over medium high heat for 2 minutes on each side. Remove cutlets to a plate. Add the remaining 2 T. butter and onions and cook until the onions become clear. Add the mushroom and cook until they begin to wilt. Add the remaining ingredients except the cutlets and bring to a boil. Add the cutlets back in, cover and let simmer 3 minutes.

Makes 2 servings.

Lamb Meatball Stroganoff

quantity	ingredient	carb grams
1 lb.	ground lamb	
1/4	medium onion, diced	4
3 t.	Italian seasoning	1
1 t.	salt	
1/2 t.	black pepper	
1 t.	garlic powder	2
1	egg slightly beaten	1
1/4 c.	dry white wine	1
2 T.	olive oil	
4 oz.	mushrooms, sliced in half	4
1 c.	sour cream	6
2 t.	paprika	2
	Total Carbohydrate Grams	21
	Carbohydrate Grams per serving	1.8

Method of Preparation:

Mix the meat, onion, egg, 2 t. of the Italian seasoning, salt, pepper and garlic powder thoroughly. Make 12 meatballs and let sit for 10 minutes. Cook the meatballs in the olive oil over medium heat until they are evenly browned. Remove from the skillet reserving as much oil as possible (you may have to add more). Cook the mushrooms over medium heat until they begin to wilt. Add the meatballs back in along with the wine, paprika and the remaining 1 t. of Italian seasoning. Cover and bring to a boil. Reduce heat and let simmer 10 minutes. Remove from the heat, remove the lid, stir in the sour cream and let it sit an additional 5 minutes.

Makes 12 servings.

Swedish Meatballs

quantity	ingredient	carb grams
1/2 lb.	ground beef	
1/2 lb.	ground pork	
1	egg beaten slightly	1
1/4	medium onion, diced	4
1 T.	dried parsley	
1/2 t.	black pepper	
1	bouillon cube	1
1/2 t.	ground allspice or nutmeg	
1 t.	garlic powder	2
1 c.	half and half	8
1/2 c.	canned beef stock	
1 t.	salt	
2 T.	butter	
	Total Carbohydrate Grams	16
	Carbohydrate Grams per serving	1.0

Method of Preparation:

Mix the meats, egg, onion, parsley, pepper, salt, 1/2 c. half and half, garlic powder and allspice or nutmeg thoroughly. Form into 16 meatballs. Fry in the butter over medium heat until well browned all over. Add the stock, bouillon cube and then the remaining 1/2 c. of half and half, cover and bring to a boil. Let simmer a couple of minutes.

Makes 16 servings.

Tortillas

suggested by Elizabeth Jackson

quantity	ingredient	carb grams
1/2 c.	soya protein isolate (soy protein powder)	
1/4 c.	soy flour	8
3	eggs slightly beaten	2
1/2 t.	salt	
1 1/2 c.	water	
	oil for cooking	
	Total Carbohydrate Grams	10
	Carbohydrate Grams per serving	1.0

Method of Preparation:

Mix all ingredients to form thin batter. Fry in about 1 T. of oil. Try to tilt pan around to make them thin. Cook until "dry" on edges, then fry on other side.

Makes 10 soft tortillas.

For chips, cut tortillas into 8 wedges and deep fry in corn oil (makes it taste like corn) until crisp. Salt while cooling.

Manicotti

Suggested by Elizabeth Jackson

quantity	ingredient	carb grams
5	Tortillas	5
1 c.	ricotta cheese	1
10 oz.	frozen spinach	12
1/3 c.	Parmesan cheese	1
1	egg slightly beaten	1
1/2 t.	nutmeg	
1/2 c.	tomato sauce	6
1/2 c.	stewed tomatoes, diced	8
1/2 t.	oregano	
1 t.	salt	
	Total Carbohydrate Grams	34
	Carbohydrate Grams per serving	6.8

Method of Preparation:

Mix cheeses, spinach, egg, salt and nutmeg. Put 1/5 of mixture on end of each tortilla and roll up. Place seam side down in greased baking dish. Mix tomatoes and sauce and pour over top. Sprinkle with oregano. Bake at 350 for about 30 minutes.

Makes 5 servings.

Cheese Garlic Biscuits

suggested by Elizabeth Jackson

quantity	ingredient	carb grams
3	eggs slightly beaten	2
1 t.	garlic powder	2
1/2 T.	dried parsley	
1 T.	dried chives	
3/4 c.	shredded cheddar cheese	4
1/4 c.	Parmesan	1
1/2 c.	soy powder (soy protein isolate)	
3 T.	sour cream	3
1/2 t.	salt	
	Total Carbohydrate Grams	12
	Carbohydrate Grams per serving	6.0

Method of Preparation:

Separate eggs. Add all remaining ingredients to egg yolks. Mix very well. Beat eggs whites until stiff. Fold into egg yolk mixture, mixing well. Divide among 6 greased muffin cups and bake in a preheated 350 degree oven for 20 minutes, or until golden brown.

Makes 6 servings.

Turkey Cutlets with Gorgonzola

quantity	ingredient	carb grams
4	turkey cutlets	
2 T.	butter	
1/4	medium onion, diced	4
1/2 c.	dry white wine	1
6 oz.	gorgonzola cheese	3
1/2 c.	sour cream	2
1/2	medium bell pepper, diced	3
1 t.	dried parsley	
1 t.	garlic powder	2
	salt and pepper to taste	
	Total Carbohydrate Grams	15
	Carbohydrate Grams per serving	7.5

Method of Preparation:

Fry the cutlets in the butter over medium hit heat until they turn white. Remove to a baking dish reserving the butter. Sprinkle the cutlets with salt and pepper. Fry the onion in the butter until it becomes clear. Stir in the peppers. Slowly add the cheese in small pieces. When the cheese is melted, add the remaining uncooked ingredients and let simmer until it becomes a creamy sauce. Pour over the cutlets and bake in a preheated oven at 300 degrees for 15 minutes.

Makes 2 servings.

Thanksgiving Turkey

Thanksgiving is my favorite meal of the year to cook. Holidays are an especially hard time to maintain your low carb eating and I'm not going to suggest that you don't go off your diet slightly. If I eat mashed potatoes and cornbread dressing only once per year, this will be the day. However, we can minimize the carbs for this day and we can make it an absolutely NO SUGAR day, as all our days should be. You have already seen the recipes for low carb vegetables and pumpkin pie (p. 211). I have no recipe for low carb mashed potatoes. Sorry. However, cooking the turkey is important. You want to make it as flavorful and as moist as possible. This is the turkey I cook every year.

quantity	ingredient	carb grams
1	turkey	
1	medium onion, sliced	
1	medium carrot, diced	
2	stalks celery, diced	
1 c.	dry white wine	
4 c.	water	
	salt and pepper to taste	
1 T.	garlic powder	
2 T.	dried parsley	
1 T.	paprika	
1 T.	onion powder	
	Total Carbohydrate Grams	
	Carbohydrate Grams per serving	1

Thanksgiving Turkey

Method of Preparation:

All of this is done on the Wednesday evening before Thanksgiving. Ensure that the turkey is properly thawed if it has been frozen. Remove the neck and the giblets from the turkey. Place your turkey in your baking pan breast side down. Ensure that you have enough room in the pan to spread the vegetables around the bottom. If you are using a baking bag, this should not be a problem. Spread the vegetables around the bottom of the pan. Pour the wine and the water over the turkey. Sprinkle the salt, pepper, garlic powder, parsley, paprika and onion powder over the turkey (whatever you have remaining just dump it in the liquid). Cover and bake in a pre-heated 400 degree oven for 30 minutes. Reduce heat to 325 degrees and plan on cooking about 20 minutes per pound or more. You will know that the turkey is cooked when you can twist the leg bone away from the thigh easily. If you have to work to do it, the bird is not cooked. Ignore the little pop-up timer if there is one. After the turkey is done cooking, turn the heat off and leave it in the oven overnight. It will still be warm the next day. On Thanksgiving day, throw away all of the vegetables in the stock. The bird will be moist and there will be plenty of stock to serve with it. If you have to count carbs in this, count it as 1 per serving for the spices.

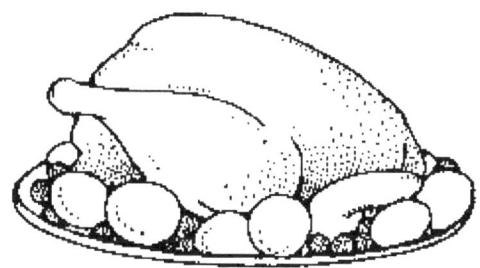

Zucchini and Crab Cakes

quantity	ingredient	carb grams
1 c.	grated zucchini	4
1/2 t.	salt	
1	can crab (about 4 oz) with liquid	
1	egg	1
2 t.	Old Bay seasoning	2
1/2 t.	Italian seasoning	
1/2 t.	salt	
3 T.	mayonnaise	
1 t.	mustard	
1/4 c.	diced onion	4
	Total Carbohydrate Grams	11
	Carbohydrate Grams per serving	5.5

Method of Preparation:

Grate zucchini and place in your mixing bowl. Sprinkle 1/2 t. salt over the zucchini and mix well. Let sit an hour in order for the salt to wilt the zucchini and draw out the water. After an hour, drain the liquid off the zucchini and squeeze it well to ensure that you get as much of the water out as possible. Combine with rest of the ingredients and let sit for 10 minutes. Make four patties. Fry in oil, covered, over medium heat until each side is well browned. It should be necessary to turn each pattie only once.

Makes 2 servings.

Vegetables

Green Beans

quantity	ingredient	carb grams
1	can (16 oz.) green beans	20
1	bouillon cube	1
1/2	medium onion, sliced	8
2 T.	butter	
	Total Carbohydrate Grams	29
	Carbohydrate Grams per serving	9.7

Method of Preparation:

Place the onion and bouillon cube in the bottom of a sauce pan. Add the green beans with the liquid and butter, bring to a boil, reduce heat and cook uncovered and stirring every five minutes. You are going to reduce the liquid to about one tablespoon. Turn off the heat and let sit 5 minutes before serving.

Makes 3 servings.

Serbian Fried Peppers

These peppers are cooked to the consistency of very thick spaghetti sauce and served as a condiment. The original recipe calls for roasting the peppers to remove the peel but we need the fiber and we don't need all of that extra work. The Serbs eat these just on good bread as a sandwich. They go as a side for any type of meat.

quantity	ingredient	carb grams
2 lb.	red bell pepper (or pimiento if you can get them), shredded or diced finely	44
1	medium onion, shredded or diced	16
1 T.	garlic powder	2
2 t.	salt	
2 t.	sugar equivalent sweetener	
4 T.	olive oil	
4 T.	white vinegar	
1/4 c.	water	
	Total Carbohydrate Grams	62
	Carbohydrate Grams per serving of 1 T.	2.6

Method of Preparation:

Put all ingredients in a heavy skillet, bring to a boil, reduce the heat and cook covered for 10 minutes. Remove the lid and stir. From this point you are going to reduce most of the liquid out of the mixture. Cook over medium heat stirring every 15 minutes. When the mixture begins to stick slightly to the pan, begin reducing heat a little at a time. You must watch it closely to prevent burning. Ultimately you will be cooking this over a low temperature barely simmering. This is finished when the volume is about 1 1/2 pints. Time of cooking is about 2 hours.

Makes about 24 servings.

Hot Cauliflower Salad (German Style)

This is modeled after the Hot German Potato Salad.

quantity	ingredient	carb grams
1 lb.	Cauliflower, cut in pieces	22
6	slices of bacon, diced	
2	stalks of celery, diced	3
1/2	medium onion, sliced	8
1 t.	salt	
1/4 c.	wine vinegar	
3/4 c.	water	
1/2 t.	black pepper	
1/2 t.	garlic powder	1
	Total Carbohydrate Grams	34
	Carbohydrate Grams per serving	8.5

Method of Preparation:

Cook your bacon over medium heat until it is well browned and the fat is rendered. Add the celery and onion and cook until the onion begins to clear. Deglaze the pan with the liquids, bring to a boil and add the spices and salt. Finally, add the cauliflower. Stir well. Cover and bring to a boil. Stir again and turn the heat off keeping the lid on. Let sit for about five minutes before serving.

Makes about 4 servings.

Rotkohl ohne Apfeln (1)

German Red Cabbage without Apples

quantity	ingredient	carb grams
1 1/2 lb.	red cabbage, shredded	36
6	slices of bacon, diced	
1/2	medium onion, sliced	8
1/2 c.	dry white wine	1
4 T.	sugar equivalent sweetener	
4 T.	wine vinegar	
1 1/2 t.	salt	
1/2 t.	caraway seeds	
	Total Carbohydrate Grams	45
	Carbohydrate Grams per serving	7.5

Method of Preparation:

Fry the bacon over medium heat until it is well browned and the fat is rendered. Add the onion and cook until it is clear. Add the remaining ingredients and bring to a boil. Reduce the heat and simmer slowly uncovered for about a half hour.

Makes about 6 servings.

Rotkohl ohne Apfeln (2)

German Sour Red Cabbage without Apples

quantity	ingredient	carb grams
2 lb.	red cabbage, shredded	48
1/4 c.	olive oil	
1/2	medium onion, sliced	8
1/2 c.	vinegar	
2 t.	salt	
1/2 t.	pepper	
1 t.	garlic powder	2
1 c.	water	
	Total Carbohydrate Grams	58
	Carbohydrate Grams per serving	7.3

Method of Preparation:

Fry the onions in the oil until they are clear. Add the cabbage and the salt and fry about 5 minutes stirring a couple of times. Add the remaining ingredients, bring to a boil and simmer covered over low heat for about an hour. Try to prepare this the day before and reheat in the microwave before serving. Will keep for several days.

Makes about 8 servings.

Hint – One tablespoon of water is equivalent to 15 cc.

English Red Cabbage

quantity	ingredient	carb grams
2 lb.	red cabbage, sliced	48
1	medium onion, sliced	16
1/2 c.	white vinegar	
2	bay leaves (leave whole)	
1/2 c.	sugar equivalent sweetener	
1/2	stick butter	
1 1/2 t.	salt	
1/2 t.	pepper	
	Total Carbohydrate Grams	64
	Carbohydrate Grams per serving	8.0

Method of Preparation:

Place everything in a pan and cover. Bring to a boil, reduce the heat and simmer at least one hour, stirring every 15 minutes. Remove the bay leaves, insuring that you get both of them, before serving.

Makes about 8 servings.

Brussel Sprouts

These might be a little high in carbs, but they are very flavorful.

quantity	ingredient	carb grams
3/4 lb.	brussel sprouts, cleaned and cut in half	24
2 T.	butter	
1/4 c.	water	
1	bouillon cube	1
1/2	medium onion, diced	8
1 t.	garlic powder	2
	Total Carbohydrate Grams	35
	Carbohydrate Grams per serving	11.7

Method of Preparation:

In a large skillet, fry the onion in the butter over medium heat until it is clear. Add the brussel sprouts and fry for about 5 minutes. Add the remaining ingredients. Bring to a boil, reduce the heat and cook, covered, 15 minutes, stirring every five minutes.

Makes 3 servings.

Yellow Crookneck Squash

quantity	ingredient	carb grams
2 lb.	yellow crookneck summer squash, sliced	34
1/2	medium onion, diced	8
3 T.	olive oil	
1 t.	salt	
1 t.	garlic powder	2
2 t.	sugar equivalent sweetener	
1/4 c.	water	
	Total Carbohydrate Grams	44
	Carbohydrate Grams per serving	11.0

Method of Preparation:

This is another of the recipes where you are going to remove most of the water from the vegetables, similar to spaghetti sauce. Place all ingredients in a large pan, cover and bring to a boil. Stir and let simmer covered about 10 minutes. Remove lid and stir. From this point on, you are going to let the water cook off, stirring every 15 minutes. Eventually it will start to stick a little to the pan. Reduce the heat slightly and continue. Ultimately, it will begin to brown a little. This is desirable. You want it to caramelize to some extent. Keep reducing the heat and stirring until the volume is about 1 quart.

Makes about 4 servings.

Sauerkraut Preparation

Sauerkraut is a very low carb friendly food. It is basically pickled cabbage. Many folks don't like sauerkraut and I contend that the reason for this is that they have never had it prepared properly. Most folks just open the can and microwave it for two minutes. This method of preparation provides for a mild but well-flavored sauerkraut and it is the sauerkraut which is referred to throughout the text. You must remember that sauerkraut must be well cooked and infused with a meat flavor.

quantity	ingredient	carb grams
1	can (16 oz.) sauerkraut	20
1	bouillon cube	1
1/2	medium onion, sliced	8
1 T.	olive oil	
3/4 c.	water	
1/2 t.	caraway seed (optional)	
1/2 t.	cayenne pepper (optional)	
1 t.	sugar equivalent sweetener (optional)	
	Total Carbohydrate Grams	29
	Carbohydrate Grams per serving	9.7

Method of Preparation:

Open the sauerkraut can retaining the lid. Over the sink, using the lid, press the juice out of the sauerkraut. You want to remove as much of the juice as possible. In a skillet, heat the oil. Add the onion and cook until it is clear. Add the kraut, the water, and the bouillon cube, bring to a boil and simmer covered for about 15 minutes. Remove the lid and reduce the liquid, stirring every ten minutes. When there is about 1/4 cup liquid remaining, remove from the heat. Let sit about 5 minutes before serving. The remaining ingredients can be added when the kraut is put into the skillet. These can be added in any combination that you think you might prefer. I like it especially with both the cayenne pepper and sweetener.

Makes about 3 servings.

Spinach and Artichoke Casserole

quantity	ingredient	carb grams
1	can (14 oz.) artichoke hearts drained	42
3	10 oz. packages frozen spinach with as much liquid as possible squeezed out.	36
8 oz.	cream cheese	6
2 T.	mayonnaise	
2 T.	olive oil	
1/4 c.	heavy cream	3
3/4 c.	Parmesan cheese	2
1 1/2 t.	salt	
1/2 t.	black pepper	
1	egg beaten	1
	Total Carbohydrate Grams	90
	Carbohydrate Grams per serving	12.9

Method of Preparation:

Oil the bottom of a 3-quart casserole with olive oil. Layer it with the artichokes. In a separate bowl, begin mixing the cream cheese, the mayonnaise and the heavy cream. When it is thoroughly mixed, mix in the remaining ingredients. When everything is well mixed pour over the artichokes. Bake at 350 degrees for 30 - 40 minutes.

Makes about 7 servings.

Baked Zucchini and Garlic

quantity	ingredient	carb grams
1 lb.	Zucchini, halved lengthwise	13
1 oz.	whole peeled garlic	9
1 t.	onion powder	1
1/2 t.	salt	
1 t.	oregano or Italian seasoning	
1/4 c.	olive oil	
	Parmesan cheese (optional)	
	mozzarella cheese (optional)	
	Total Carbohydrate Grams	23
	Carbohydrate Grams per serving	7.7

Method of Preparation:

Mix everything (except cheeses) in a bowl to ensure even coating. Place on a baking sheet and bake at 325 degrees for 30 minutes. If the garlic isn't quite soft, continue cooking checking every 5 minutes. Can cover with mozzarella and/or Parmesan and brown.

Makes about 3 servings.

Kim-Chee

Kim-chee is very flavorful, but it is also very spicy (hot) and if you make it at home, the odor can run you out of the kitchen. You can now buy this in many groceries if you don't want to make it. It is very low carb.

quantity	ingredient	carb grams
1	head Chinese cabbage (2 - 2 1/2 lb.)	5
1/4 c.	salt	
2 T.	crushed red hot peppers	2
1 bunch	scallions	4
1 T.	garlic powder	6
1 t.	ginger	1
	Total Carbohydrate Grams	18
	Carbohydrate Grams per serving of 2 oz.	1.1

Method of Preparation:

Remove the bottom of the cabbage. Cut it into one inch lengths. Wash and drain. Sprinkle the salt thoroughly over the cabbage. Let sit for about 4 hours. Drain and wash once with cold water. Dice the bottom half of each scallion. Add it and the rest of the ingredients to the bruised cabbage and mix well. Let sit for 24 hours. Refrigerate, mixing at least once daily. Can start eating immediately but it tastes better the longer it is allowed to sit. It starts tasting its best after at least 2 days in the refrigerator. Will keep several weeks. For variations add 1/2 cup of dried shrimp.

Makes 16 servings.

American Cabbage Kim-Chee

quantity	ingredient	carb grams
2 1/2 lb.	Cabbage, cut to bite size pieces	50
1/4 c.	salt	
1 T.	garlic powder	6
2 t.	sugar equivalent sweetener	
1 1/2 t.	seedless crushed red pepper	1
1/2	medium onion, sliced thinly	8
1 t.	ginger	
	Total Carbohydrate Grams	53
	Carbohydrate Grams per serving	2.7

Method of Preparation:

Mix salt and cabbage thoroughly. Let sit 6 to 8 hours. Wash with cold water once and drain. Add garlic, pepper, onion, mix well, and let sit 24 hours. Mix in sugar and refrigerate, mixing at least once daily. Can eat immediately but will start tasting best after three days. Will keep several weeks.

Makes about 20 servings.

Hint – One pint of water is equivalent to one pound.

Cucumber Kim-Chee

quantity	ingredient	carb grams
2 1/2 lb.	medium cucumbers	23
1 bunch	scallions	4
1/4 c.	salt	
1 1/2 T.	seedless dried red peppers	3
1 T.	garlic powder	6
	Total Carbohydrate Grams	36
	Carbohydrate Grams per serving	1.8

Method of Preparation:

If the cucumbers were purchased from the grocery store they must be peeled. Slice them to about 1/8-inch thickness. If the seeds are hard they must be removed. Mix well with the salt and let sit for about 4 hours. Wash once with cold water. Remove the roots from the scallions, wash, and dice the bottom half of each scallion. Mix the onions and the rest of the ingredients with the bruised cucumbers and let sit for 24 hours. Refrigerate and mix at least once daily. They are ready to eat immediately but will taste better after sitting at least three days. Will keep at least 2 weeks

Makes about 20 servings.

Pickled Garlic and Garlic Shoots

(Korean "Manu Tsung A Chee")

quantity	ingredient	carb grams
2 T.	cider vinegar	
4 T.	soy sauce	
3 T.	sugar equivalent sweetener	
1	heaping cup cleaned garlic cloves and stems	30
	Total Carbohydrate Grams	30
	Carbohydrate Grams per serving	3.8

Method of Preparation:

Mix vinegar, soy sauce and sugar in a covered pan and bring to a boil. Add the garlic, let it come to a boil again, simmer covered about 2 minutes and then turn off the heat. Let sit until cool. Put in a jar. Refrigerate the next day. Ready in about two weeks. Will keep refrigerated several weeks. Serve only the garlic buds and stems. Serve about 1 ounce per person. Reserve the liquid for making Bar-B-Q or chicken wings.

Makes about 8 servings.

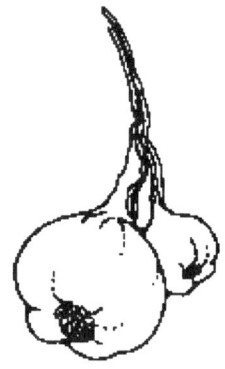

Wilted Bean Sprouts

quantity	ingredient	carb grams
3 c.	bean sprouts	18
1 t.	salt	
1 t.	garlic powder	2
1 T	sesame oil	
	Total Carbohydrate Grams	20
	Carbohydrate Grams per serving	3.3

Method of Preparation:

Place bean sprouts in a basket. Wash them in boiling water until they wilt slightly, then put them in cold water to stop the cooking. Drain well. Add salt and garlic and mix. Add the oil, mix well, and refrigerate. Serve cold, about 1/2 cup per person. This will not keep more than a few days.

Makes about 6 servings.

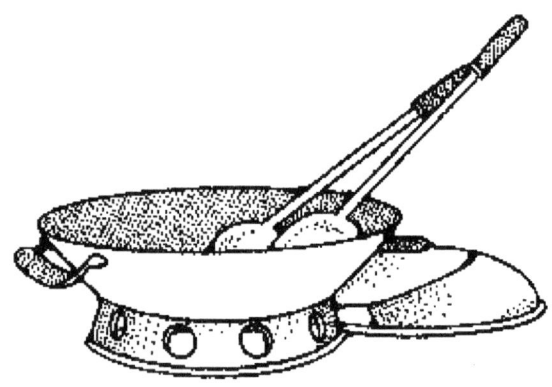

Wilted Spinach

quantity	ingredient	carb grams
3/4 lb.	fresh spinach	12
1 t.	salt	
1 t.	garlic powder	2
1 T.	sesame oil	
1 T.	sesame seeds	2
	Total Carbohydrate Grams	16
	Carbohydrate Grams per serving	1.6

Method of Preparation:

Wash the spinach. Rinse in boiling water until the spinach is slightly wilted then rinse in cold water to stop the cooking. Mix in the dry ingredients, then the oil. Refrigerate. Serve about 1 ounce per person.

Makes about 10 servings.

Hint – The list of hidden sugars includes: carob, corn syrup, dextrin, dextrose, dulcitol, fructose, glucose, glucerol, honey, lactose, levulose, maltose, maltodextrin, manitol, mannose, molasses, saccharose, sorbitol, sorghum, treacle, turbinado, xylotol, glycerin and xylose.

Wilted Zucchini

quantity	ingredient	carb grams
1 lb.	medium to small zucchini, sliced thinly	13
1/4	medium onion, sliced thinly	4
1 t.	garlic powder	2
2 T.	sesame oil	
1 T.	sesame seeds	2
1 t.	salt	
	Total Carbohydrate Grams	21
	Carbohydrate Grams per serving	1.3

Method of Preparation:

Wilt zucchini and onion in boiling water. Cool under cold water to stop the cooking. Squeeze out the liquid. Mix in the rest of the ingredients and let sit 2 - 3 hours. Serve chilled.

Makes about 16 servings.

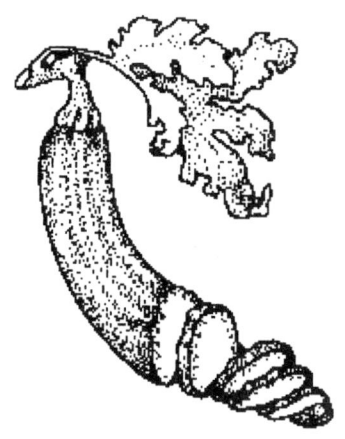

Eggs

Basic Scrambled Eggs

quantity	ingredient	carb grams
3	eggs	2
3 T.	half and half	
1/8 t.	salt	
1/4 t.	onion powder	
1/4 t.	garlic powder	
	pinch black pepper	
2 T.	olive oil or butter	
	cheese (optional)	
	ham, bacon, sausage or deli sausages (optional)	
	bell pepper (optional)	
	mushrooms (optional)	
	salsa (p. 236, optional)	
	Total Carbohydrate Grams	2
	Carbohydrate Grams per serving	2

Method of Preparation:

Place everything in a bowl and mix well with a fork. In a skillet over medium high heat, if you have vegetables and or meat, cook this first in the olive oil. Add the eggs and continue stirring until they are only slightly runny. Plate the mixture. At this point you can add the cheese and heat in a microwave for 15 seconds. Try to limit anything that you add to the eggs to under 1/2 cup. In other words, you want more eggs than additions. Make sure you add in any additional carbs.

Makes 1 serving.

Frittata/One Skillet Quiche

Omelets are wonderful for the low carb eater, but they are a little harder to cook than just plain old scrambled eggs and options because they have to be flipped. The Italian frittata is an omelet which doesn't have to be turned. It is steamed and is, therefore, easier to prepare. Frittata can be converted to a "crustless pie" by pouring into a greased baking dish and baking at 325 degrees (for one helping) for about 40 minutes. A crust can be made of crushed pork rinds if you so desire.

Quiche Lorraine Frittata

quantity	ingredient	carb grams
1	recipe Basic Scrambled Eggs (p. 199)	2
1/2 t.	nutmeg	
1 oz.	Parmesan cheese	1
6	slices of bacon, diced	
1/2	medium onion, diced	8
2 oz.	Swiss cheese, diced	1
	Total Carbohydrate Grams	12
	Carbohydrate Grams per serving	12

Method of Preparation:

Fry the bacon over medium heat until it is well browned. Add the onion and cook until they are clear. Remove from heat and let cool. After this has cooled, mix it with the eggs, nutmeg and Parmesan cheese and mix thoroughly. Heat your egg skillet over medium heat. Add the cooking oil. Mix, again, your egg mixture and pour it into the skillet. Add the Swiss cheese and cover. Reduce the heat to low. Cook until the mixture is soft but solid on top. Remove to your plate.

Makes one serving.

Chicken and Broccoli Frittata

quantity	ingredient	carb grams
2	recipes Basic Scrambled Eggs (p. 199)	4
1/2 t.	nutmeg	
1 oz.	Parmesan cheese	1
4 oz.	chicken, diced	
1/4	medium onion, diced	4
2 oz.	Swiss cheese, diced	1
1 c.	broccoli, chopped	8
	red pepper sauce to taste (a shake or two)	
2 T.	olive oil	
	Total Carbohydrate Grams	18
	Carbohydrate Grams per serving	9

Method of Preparation:

Fry the onions in 2 T. oil over medium heat until they become clear. Add broccoli and chicken and cook until broccoli begins to wilt. Let cool. Mix with egg mixture, nutmeg, red sauce and Parmesan cheese. Heat 2 T. oil in your egg skillet over medium heat. Add the egg mixture to the skillet, sprinkle with the Swiss cheese, cover and reduce the heat to low. Cook until the mixture is not runny.

Makes two servings.

Shrimp Quiche

quantity	ingredient	carb grams
2	recipes Basic Scrambled Eggs (p. 199)	4
1/2 c.	sour cream	3
8 oz.	salad shrimp (2 cans very small shrimp reserve the juice)	
1/4	medium onion, diced	4
1/2 c.	chopped green chilies	4
1/2 c.	colby cheese, diced	2
1/2 c.	monterey jack cheese, diced	2
2 T.	butter	
1/4 c.	Salsa for serving (p. 236)	3
	Total Carbohydrate Grams	22
	Carbohydrate Grams per serving	11.0

Method of Preparation:

Mix the eggs, sour cream, shrimp, chilies and cheeses. Cook the onion in the oil over medium high heat until it become clear. Pour the egg mixture into the pan, cover and reduce the heat to low. Cook until the mixture is soft but solid on top. Remove to your plate. Spoon the salsa over the top.

Makes two servings.

Hint – One pound is equivalent to 454 grams of water.

Spinach Quiche

quantity	ingredient	carb grams
2	recipes Basic Scrambled Eggs (p. 199)	4
1/2 t.	nutmeg	
3 oz.	Parmesan cheese	1
1 T.	lemon juice	
1/4	medium onion, diced	4
10 oz.	frozen spinach with juice squeezed out	12
2 T.	butter	
	Total Carbohydrate Grams	21
	Carbohydrate Grams per serving	10.5

Method of Preparation:

Mix the nutmeg, Parmesan cheese, lemon juice and spinach with the eggs. Fry the onion in the butter over medium high heat until the onion becomes clear. Pour the egg mixture into the pan, cover and reduce the heat to low. Cook until the mixture is soft but solid on top. Remove to your plate.

Makes two servings.

German Quiche

quantity	ingredient	carb grams
2	recipe Basic Scrambled Eggs (p. 199)	4
1/2 t.	nutmeg	
1/2 t.	oregano	
1 oz.	Parmesan cheese	1
4 oz.	ham	
1/4	medium onion, diced	4
2 oz.	Swiss cheese, diced	1
1 c.	cooked cauliflower, chopped	8
1/2 c.	sour cream	3
2 T.	olive oil	
	Total Carbohydrate Grams	21
	Carbohydrate Grams per serving	11.5

Method of Preparation:

Mix the eggs, nutmeg, oregano, Parmesan, ham, sour cream and Swiss cheese. Fry the onions in the oil and cauliflower over medium high heat until the onions become clear. Pour the egg mixture into the pan, cover and reduce the heat to low. Cook until the mixture is soft but solid on top. Remove to your plate.

Makes 2 servings.

Salmon Quiche

quantity	ingredient	carb grams
2	recipes Basic Scrambled Eggs (p. 199)	4
1/2 t.	dill weed	
8 oz.	canned salmon	
1/4	medium onion, diced	4
4 oz.	Swiss cheese, diced	1
1/2 c.	sour cream	8
2 T.	olive oil	
	Total Carbohydrate Grams	17
	Carbohydrate Grams per serving	8.5

Method of Preparation:

Mix the eggs, dill, salmon, sour cream and Swiss cheese. Fry the onions in the oil over medium high heat until they become clear. Pour the egg mixture into the pan, cover and reduce the heat to low. Cook until the mixture is soft but solid on top. Remove to your plate.

Makes two servings.

Cheddar Chili Frittata

quantity	ingredient	carb grams
2	recipes Scrambled Eggs (p. 199)	2
2 T.	butter	
1/2 c.	shredded cheddar cheese	2
6 oz.	sliced ham, diced	
1/2 c.	sour cream	3
1/4	medium onion, diced	4
2 T.	pickled jalapeño peppers, diced	1
	Total Carbohydrate Grams	12
	Carbohydrate Grams per serving	6

Method of Preparation:

Mix the eggs, cheese, ham, sour cream and jalapeños. Fry the onions in the oil over medium high heat until they become clear. Pour the egg mixture into the pan, cover and reduce the heat to low. Cook until the mixture is soft but solid on top. Remove to your plate.

Makes two servings.

Hint – Yes, whipping cream does have carbs, about 0.6 grams per tablespoon.

Egg Salad

Egg salad is typically composed of hard-boiled eggs, mayonnaise, mustard, salt, pepper and additions. The additions can include such things as onion, garlic, pickles, peppers, ham, bacon, various deli meats, etc. Below is an example. By the way, this makes a wonderful breakfast.

quantity	ingredient	carb grams
6	hard boiled eggs, diced finely	4
2	stalks celery, diced	3
1/4 c.	Pickled Onions (p. 216)	4
1/2 t.	garlic powder	1
1/4 t.	salt	
1/8 t.	black pepper	
1/4 lb.	Genoa salami, diced	
1 t.	Dijon mustard	
1/4 c.	mayonnaise	
	Total Carbohydrate Grams	12
	Carbohydrate Grams per serving	6.0

Method of Preparation:

Mix all ingredients and refrigerate until ready to serve.

Makes about 2 servings.

Eggs Stuffed with Crab Meat

quantity	ingredient	carb grams
6	cooled hard boiled eggs peeled	4
3/4 c.	cooked crab meat flaked	
2	stalks celery, diced finely	3
1 t.	dry mustard	
1/2 t.	onion powder	
1/2 t.	garlic powder	2
1/8 t.	salt	
1 pinch	black pepper	
1/3 c.	mayonnaise	
	paprika for garnish	
	Total Carbohydrate Grams	9
	Carbohydrate Grams per serving	0.8

Method of Preparation:

Cut the eggs in half lengthwise. Remove the yolks to a bowl. Mix everything with the yolks. Spoon the mixture into the egg whites, sprinkle with paprika and refrigerate until needed.

Makes 12 servings.

Green Chili Eggs

quantity	ingredient	carb grams
2 - 3	frozen whole green chilies, seeded and wiped dry	1
1 lb.	grated Monterrey jack cheese	8
12	eggs	8
16 oz.	sour cream	12
1/2 t.	salt	
1/4 t.	pepper	
1 t.	garlic powder	2
1 t.	onion powder	1
	Total Carbohydrate Grams	32
	Carbohydrate Grams per serving	8.0

Method of Preparation:

Layer the chilies with the grated cheese in a buttered or greased 13x9x2 inch baking dish, combine the eggs and all other ingredients and pour over the top. Bake for 30 minutes in a 350 degree oven until it puffs like a soufflé.

Makes 4 servings.

Boiling and Peeling Eggs

As low carb eaters, we can eat a lot of boiled eggs. There are better and worse methods to boil and peel eggs. These suggestions come from the American Egg Board in their *Eggcyclopedia, 3rd edition.*

Egg Selection - (If possible) Select eggs which are neither too fresh nor too old - eggs that have been refrigerated a week to ten days. Eggs should be stored small-end up for 24 hours before boiling in order to center the yolk.

Boiling - Pierce the shells before cooking. Place the eggs in a single layer at the bottom of a pan. Cover the eggs with cold water an inch above the eggs. Add 2 to 4 tablespoons of salt per gallon of water. Bring the water to a boil quickly, let simmer five minutes and remove from heat. Let sit an additional 10 minutes (for large eggs. Subtract 3 minutes for medium eggs and an additional 3 minutes for small eggs) in the hot water. Cool the eggs as quickly as possible; under cold running water for 5 minutes is suggested.

Peeling - If the eggs aren't going to be used immediately, refrigerate in the shell in the carton for up to a week. Otherwise, crack the shell all over by tapping gently on the counter, then roll the egg around in your palm. Begin peeling with the large end. Holding the egg under water or dipping it in water facilitates the peeling.

Desserts

Pumpkin Pie

quantity	ingredient	carb grams
1	can (16 oz.) pumpkin	40
2	eggs	1
3 c.	sugar equivalent sweetener	
1/2 t.	salt	
3 T.	pumpkin pie spice	9
1 c.	half and half	8
1 T.	olive oil	
	Total Carbohydrate Grams	58
	Carbohydrate Grams per serving	9.7

Method of Preparation:

Heat the half and half and sweetener in a microwave about 1 minute giving the sweetener a chance to dissolve. Let cool. Beat the eggs well. Add the oil and blend well. Add the pumpkin, the salt, the spices and mix thoroughly. Add the half and half and mix well. Oil your baking pan. Bake in a preheated oven at 400 degrees for 20 minutes. Reduce heat to 325 degrees and bake about 50 minutes or until a knife inserted in the center of the pie comes out clean. The top will fell "firm" to the touch.

Makes 6 servings.

Pumpkin Mousse Pie

quantity	ingredient	carb grams
1 c.	canned pumpkin	20
1/2 c.	half and half	4
3 c.	sugar equivalent sweetener	
1 t.	cinnamon	
1/4 t.	nutmeg	
1/8 t.	ginger	
1 t.	vanilla	
1 T.	(1 envelope) gelatin	
1/2 c.	boiling water	
1/4 c.	ice water	
	dried egg whites - 3 egg equivalent	
	Total Carbohydrate Grams	24
	Carbohydrate Grams per serving	4.0

Method of Preparation:

Combine the pumpkin, half-and-half, spices, vanilla and sweetener. Stir the gelatin into the boiling water until it is dissolved, then add the ice water. Let cool to room temperature and add to the pumpkin mixture. Follow the instructions on the box of egg whites for the equivalent of 3 egg whites. Beat the egg whites and fold into the pumpkin mixture. Put in a pie pan and chill until firm.

Makes 6 servings.

Wine Syllabub

suggested by Crystal Feist

quantity	ingredient	carb grams
6 T.	dry white wine	1
1/2 c	sugar equivalent sweetener	
3 T.	lemon juice	3
1 T.	brandy	1
1 t.	grated lemon peel	
1/8 t.	nutmeg	
1 c.	whipped cream	6
	fresh berries for serving (optional)	
	Total Carbohydrate Grams	11
	Carbohydrate Grams per serving	2.8

Method of Preparation:

Combine wine, sweetener, lemon juice, brandy and lemon peel in a bowl and let marinade as long as possible, at least a couple of hours at room temperature or refrigerated overnight. Whip the cream to stiff peaks stage. Fold in the marinade gently 2 T. at a time. Spoon into 4 wine glasses and refrigerate until serving. Garnish with berries.

Makes 4 servings.

Pancakes

suggested by Elizabeth Jackson

quantity	ingredient	carb grams
1/2 c.	soy protein powder	
1/4 c.	soy flour	8
3	eggs beaten	2
3/4 c.	water	
1/4 c.	heavy cream	2
1/4 t.	salt	
1 t.	baking powder	
	oil for the griddle/skillet	
	butter for serving	
	low carb syrup for serving	
	Total Carbohydrate Grams	12
	Carbohydrate Grams per serving	1.3

Method of Preparation:

Mix all ingredients in blender. Cook in a lightly oiled skillet over medium heat until browned on both sides. The texture improves after freezing, so you can double the recipe and make them ahead of time.

Makes 9 pancakes.

Chocolate Drop Cookies
suggested by Elizabeth Jackson

quantity	ingredient	carb grams
3/4 c.	sugar equivalent sweetener	
1/2 c.	butter softened to room temperature	
2	eggs beaten slightly	1
1 oz.	melted unsweetened chocolate	8
1/2 c.	water	
1 t.	vanilla	3
1 c.	soy flour	32
1/2 c.	soy protein powder	
1/2 t.	baking soda	
1/2 t.	salt	
1 c.	chopped walnuts	15
	Total Carbohydrate Grams	59
	Carbohydrate Grams per serving	1.4

Method of Preparation:

Mix 1st 6 ingredients. Add next 5 ingredients and mix well. Stir in nuts. Drop by rounded teaspoons onto ungreased cookie sheet. Bake at 375 degrees for 10 minutes. These cookies must sit in a covered dish or plastic bag refrigerated overnight before eating.

Make 3 1/2 dozen cookies.

Other/Basic Recipes

Pickled Onions

These are a staple for my salads. They are milder than vidalia onions.
Count their carbs as you would regular onions. These are used in many
other recipes.

quantity	ingredient	carb grams
3 lb.	onions, diced and/or sliced	96
2 3/4 c.	water	
7/8 c.	white vinegar	
2 T.	salt	
3 T.	sugar equivalent sweetener	
	Total Carbohydrate Grams	96
	Carbohydrate Grams per serving of 1 T.	0.7

Method of Preparation:

Slice or dice the onions with a stainless steel knife and pack them
tightly in 2 quart jars (an old mayonnaise jar works nicely). Place the
sweetener on top of the onions. Bring the remaining ingredients to a
boil and pour them over the onions. Let these cool to room temperature
and close with a regular lid. Place in the refrigerator. They are ready
the next day. These must be kept refrigerated and will keep several
months. This recipe can easily be halved.

Makes 2 quarts.

Sweet Pickle Relish

This is used in several recipes, but it takes only a couple of days to "make". Try to use pickling cucumbers if they are available (if you can find them; they don't have to be peeled). This doesn't look like "store bought" relish because, among other reasons, the cucumbers are peeled and there is no added food coloring. It does, however, have good flavor. One variation on this is to use zucchini squash rather than cucumbers.

quantity	ingredient	carb grams
1 lb.	cucumbers, peeled and diced or shredded	9
1/2 c.	water	
1/2 c.	vinegar	
1 t.	mustard seed	
1 1/2 t.	salt	
5 T.	sugar equivalent sweetener	
	Total Carbohydrate Grams	9
	Carbohydrate Grams per serving of 1 T.	0.3

Method of Preparation:

Bring all ingredients except the cucumbers to a boil and remove from heat. In the meantime, pack the cucumbers tightly in a pint jar. Pour the hot liquid over the cucumbers and let sit until they are room temperature. Put on the lid and refrigerate. These are ready after a couple of days. They should be kept refrigerated and they will keep several months.

Makes 16 servings.

Chow Chow

quantity	ingredient	carb grams
1 lb.	cabbage, shredded	18
1/2	medium onion, diced finely	8
1/2	medium bell pepper, diced finely	3
2 oz.	tomato sauce	3
1/2 t.	red pepper flakes	
1/2 c.	water	
3/4 c.	vinegar	
1 t.	mustard seed	1
1 t.	celery seed	1
1 t.	garlic powder	2
2 t.	salt	
6 T.	sugar equivalent sweetener	
	Total Carbohydrate Grams	36
	Carbohydrate Grams per serving of 1 T.	0.6

Method of Preparation:

Bring all ingredients to a boil stirring a couple of times and remove from heat. Let cool and pack in a quart jar.

Makes about 1 quart.

Ketchup

One of the first things folks complained about was not having ketchup. This recipe has a lot of flavor and is relatively quick to make. Note the subtle combination of sweet and sour flavor.

quantity	ingredient	carb grams
2 1/2 c.	tomato sauce	30
1 c.	water	
1/2	medium onion, diced	8
1 T.	garlic powder	6
2 T.	olive oil	
1/2 c.	cider vinegar	
5 T.	sugar equivalent sweetener	
1 T.	salt	
2 t.	dry mustard	2
1 ½ t.	cinnamon	1
	Total Carbohydrate Grams	47
	Carbohydrate Grams per serving of 1 T.	0.7

Method of Preparation:

In a heavy sauce pan, over medium heat, add the oil and the onion and cook until the onions are clear. Add the remaining ingredients. Reduce the heat to low and cook for about 30 minutes. Pour into a jar or freezer container and let cool. This ketchup should keep in your refrigerator for at least a week. Refrigerate or freeze the rest until it is needed. If you freeze it, you might want to put it in an ice cube tray or something else which is portioned so you don't have to thaw and refreeze the whole batch each time you want ketchup.

Makes 4 cups.

Chili Sauce

Chili Sauce is very similar to ketchup. It has the added hot flavor along with the sweet and sour combination.

quantity	ingredient	carb grams
2 1/2 c.	tomato sauce	30
1 c.	water	
1/2	medium onion, diced	8
1	medium bell pepper, diced	6
2	jalapeño peppers, diced (use fresh or canned)	2
1 stalk	celery, diced	1
1 T.	garlic powder	2
3 T.	oil	
3/4 c.	cider vinegar	
1/2 c.	sugar equivalent sweetener	
4 t.	salt	
2 t.	dry mustard	2
2 t.	cinnamon	2
1 t.	grated nutmeg	1
1 t.	cloves	1
1 t.	ground allspice	1
	Total Carbohydrate Grams	56
	Carbohydrate Grams per serving of 1 T.	0.7

Chili Sauce

Method of Preparation:

In a heavy sauce pan, over medium heat, add the oil and the onion, the celery and the peppers and cook until the onions are clear. Add the remaining ingredients. Reduce the heat to low and cook for about 30 minutes. Pour into a jar or freezer container and let cool. This is your chili sauce. In other recipes in this book which call for the inclusion of Chili Sauce, use this chili sauce. Refrigerate or freeze the rest until it is needed. If you freeze it, you might want to put it in an ice cube tray or something else which is portioned so you don't have to thaw and refreeze the whole batch each time you want chili sauce.

Makes about 5 cups.

Worcestershire Sauce

quantity	ingredient	carb grams
1 1/4 c.	water	
1/2 c.	vinegar	
1/4 c.	soy sauce	
1/2 c.	Thai fish sauce (made with anchovies)	
1 t.	cloves	1
1 t.	garlic powder	2
1 t.	onion powder	1
1 t.	cayenne pepper	1
3 T.	sugar equivalent sweetener	
	Total Carbohydrate Grams	5
	Carbohydrate Grams per serving of 1T.	0.1

Method of Preparation:

In a pan, bring the water to a boil. Turn it off. Add the spices and stir. Add the other liquids and stir. Add the sweetener and stir. Let sit overnight refrigerated with everything still combined. You can then strain this through a coffee filter to reduce the carbs even further if you want to.

Makes 2 1/2 cups.

Faux Balsamic Vinegar

For those of you who like the flavor of balsamic vinegar but don't want the carbs to go along with it (and there might be one or two of you out there), buy some good wine vinegar and sweeten it yourself. I put the equivalent of 1 teaspoon of sugar (again, more or less depending on your taste) per ounce of vinegar. I use this mostly for salads and occasionally for cooking.

12 oz. bottle red wine vinegar
4 T. sugar equivalent sweetener

Method of Preparation:

Mix the vinegar and sweetener thoroughly in the vinegar jar. Ready in about ten minutes.

For flavored vinegars, which are good to give as presents, you need ½ cup of fruit and enough white vinegar to make one pint. Do not use cider vinegar because, according to the USDA, it has 0.9 grams of carbs per tablespoon in and of itself. Bring one cup of vinegar to a boil in a covered pan. Add the fruit, stir and bring to a boil again. Turn off the heat and let cool to room temperature. Mash the fruit to ensure that there is as much surface area exposed to the vinegar as possible. Basically, you are going to pickle the fruit and then throw the fruit away reserving the liquid. At the end of a week, strain the liquid from the solids and discard the solids. Add enough white vinegar or white wine vinegar to make a pint and store in a pint jar. A pint is equal to 32 servings of one tablespoon each. We must assume that all available carbs in the fruit goes into the vinegar solution. The carb counts are given below for the various fruits. Use as you would plain vinegar. When used in a salad, don't dilute with any water.

Strawberries – 3.6 total grams of available carbs or 0.1 grams carbs per T.

Blackberries – 5.4 total grams of available carbs or 0.2 grams carbs per T.

Blueberries – 8.3 total grams of available carbs or 0.3 grams carbs per T.

Cranberries – 4.7 total grams of available carbs or 0.2 grams carbs per T.

Raspberries – 2.9 total grams of available carbs or 0.1 grams carbs per T.

Basic Bar-B-Q Sauce

This Bar-B-Q Sauce is very similar to our ketchup. This has a larger contrast of flavors than the Chili Sauce and different spices.

quantity	ingredient	carb grams
2 1/2 c.	tomato sauce	30
1 c.	water	
2 T.	onion powder	2
2 T.	garlic powder	4
4 t.	salt	
2 t.	dry mustard	
2 t.	black pepper	2
4 t.	dried red pepper flakes	2
3 T.	oil	
1 c.	cider vinegar	
3/4 c.	sugar equivalent sweetener	
	Total Carbohydrate Grams	40
	Carbohydrate Grams per serving of 1 T.	0.7

Method of Preparation:

In a heavy sauce pan, over medium heat, add all of the ingredients. Bring to a boil, reduce the heat to low and cook for about 30 minutes. Pour into a jar or freezer container and let cool. This is your Bar-B-Q sauce. Refrigerate or freeze the rest until it is needed. Add more or less red pepper to modify hotness. Can be diluted with Ketchup (p. 219) if your first attempt is too hot.

Makes about 5 cups.

Mexican Bar-B-Q Sauce

quantity	ingredient	carb grams
1/3 c.	sugar equivalent sweetener	
6 T.	chili powder	24
2 t.	cayenne pepper (optional for hotness)	2
1/4 c.	Ketchup (p. 219)	3
1/4 c.	cider vinegar	
2 T.	olive oil	
2 T.	dry mustard	2
1/2 t.	salt	
1 T.	hot pepper sauce (optional for hotness)	1
	Total Carbohydrate Grams	32
	Carbohydrate Grams per serving of 1 T.	2.7

Method of Preparation:

Bring all ingredients to a boil in a sauce pan, reduce heat and simmer 10 minutes covered. Taste and adjust for "hotness".

Makes about 3/4 cup.

Texas Bar-B-Q Sauce

quantity	ingredient	carb grams
1 c.	Ketchup (p. 219)	10
2 T.	Worcestershire Sauce (p. 222)	
1/2 c.	sugar equivalent sweetener	
1/4 c.	lime juice	9
2 T.	red pepper flakes	1
1 t.	salt	
2 T.	olive oil	
1/2	medium onion, diced	8
2 T.	canned jalapeño or chipotle pepper, diced	2
1 T.	garlic powder	6
6 oz.	tomato paste	30
12 oz.	low carb light beer	3
	Total Carbohydrate Grams	69
	Carbohydrate Grams per serving of 1 T.	1.4

Method of Preparation:

Fry the onion in a sauce pan until it is clear.   Add remaining ingredients except the tomato paste, cover, and bring to a boil. Reduce heat, and simmer 20 minutes. Thicken with the tomato paste, and simmer an additional 10 minutes.

Makes about 3 cups.

French Style Bar-B-Q Sauce

Use this as a basting sauce for your meat as you grill it and as a dipping sauce.

quantity	ingredient	carb grams
1/3 c.	sugar equivalent sweetener	
1/3 c.	dry white wine	1
1/3 c.	white wine vinegar	
1/3 c.	olive oil	
1/4 c.	Dijon mustard	8
1 T.	dried parsley	
2 t.	garlic powder	4
3/4 t.	salt	
1/2 t.	white pepper	
1/2 c.	onions, diced	8
	Total Carbohydrate Grams	21
	Carbohydrate Grams per serving of 1 T.	0.9

Method of Preparation:

Sauté your onions in the oil until they are clear. Add remaining ingredients, cover, bring to a boil, and simmer for about 15 minutes.

Makes about 1 1/2 cups.

Cocktail Sauce

quantity	ingredient	carb grams
1 c.	Chili Sauce (p. 220)	10
1 T.	Worcestershire Sauce (p. 222)	
1 T.	lemon juice	1
1 t.	horseradish	1
	Total Carbohydrate Grams	12
	Carbohydrate Grams per serving of 1 T.	0.7

Method of Preparation:

Mix all ingredients. Let sit 10 minutes before serving.

Makes about 18 servings.

Tartar Sauce

quantity	ingredient	carb grams
1 c.	mayonnaise	
1/4 c.	Pickled Onions (p. 216)	4
1/4 c.	Sweet Pickle Relish (p. 217)	3
2 T.	lemon juice	2
	Total Carbohydrate Grams	9
	Carbohydrate Grams per serving of 1 T.	0.4

Method of Preparation:

Mix all ingredients and refrigerate.

Makes 25 servings.

Hint – Walnuts, almonds, macadamia nuts and Brazil nuts are good sources for fat and fiber and are good sources for adjusting your daily calories. Peanuts and cashews tend to have more carbs and should be used with caution.

Spicy Indian Crab Dip

A dip for low carbohydrate vegetables or perhaps to top an omelet

quantity	ingredient	carb grams
1/2 c.	sour cream	3
2 T.	Worcestershire Sauce (p. 222)	
4	scallions, chopped finely	2
1	can (4 oz.) crab	
1 pkt.	dried onion soup mix	4
2 t.	curry powder	1
1/2 t.	cayenne pepper (very optional)	1
1/2 t.	black pepper	
	Total Carbohydrate Grams	11
	Carbohydrate Grams per serving of 1 T.	0.7

Method of Preparation:

Mix all ingredients until well combined. Chill for 2 hours before serving

Makes 1 cup.

Cajun Seasoning

In a bowl, mix equal parts of black pepper, red cayenne pepper, garlic powder, onion powder, paprika, Italian seasoning or oregano, and salt. Count this as 1 gram carb per teaspoon.

Hint – The list of hidden sugars includes: carob, corn syrup, dextrin, dextrose, dulcitol, fructose, glucose, glucerol, honey, lactose, levulose, maltose, maltodextrin, manitol, mannose, molasses, saccharose, sorbitol, sorghum, treacle, turbinado, xylotol, glycerin and xylose.

Green Chile & Lime Sauce

quantity	ingredient	carb grams
2 T.	lime juice	4
1 c.	mayonnaise	
2	green chilies, diced	2
1/4 t.	salt	
1/2 t.	garlic powder	1
	Total Carbohydrate Grams	7
	Carbohydrate Grams per serving of 1 T.	0.5

Method of Preparation:

In your mixing bowl, combine the lime juice, the chilies and the salt. Let them marinate an hour. Blend in the mayonnaise. Serve with fish, fish cakes, etc.

Makes about 1 cup.

Hint – One ounce of water is equivalent to two tablespoons.

Yaki Mandu Sauce

This Korean type sauce is normally served with Yaki Mandu, a meat dumpling wrapped in noodle dough. We can't have the noodle dough, but we can have the sauce.

quantity	ingredient	carb grams
3/4 c.	soy sauce	
1/4 c.	vinegar	
1/2 t.	red pepper	
1/4 c.	sugar equivalent sweetener	
2 t.	chives	
1 t.	sesame seeds	1
	Total Carbohydrate Grams	
	Carbohydrate Grams per serving	0

Method of Preparation:

Heat first three ingredients. Add last three ingredients. Let cool. Use with other recipes as noted.

Makes about 1 cup.

Thai Hot Sauce

quantity	ingredient	carb grams
2 T.	dried shrimp, diced finely	
1 T.	garlic powder	6
1 T.	red pepper flakes	1
2 t.	sugar equivalent sweetener	
3 T.	Nam Pla fish sauce	
3 T.	lime juice	3
2 T.	pickled jalapeño peppers, diced	2
	Total Carbohydrate Grams	12
	Carbohydrate Grams per serving of 1 T.	1

Method of Preparation:

Dissolve the sweetener in the lime juice. Blend all ingredients into a paste.

Makes about 3/4 c.

Hint – a tablespoon is equivalent to three teaspoons.

Guacamole

quantity	ingredient	carb grams
2 c.	avocados	34
2 T.	sour cream	1
1 t.	garlic powder	2
1/2 t.	salt	
1/4 c.	green chilies, diced	2
1 T.	lemon juice	1
1/2 t.	Tabasco sauce	
1/4 c.	Pickled Onions (p. 216)	4
1	small tomato seeds removed and diced	4
1/2 t.	sugar equivalent sweetener	
	Total Carbohydrate Grams	48
	Carbohydrate Grams per serving of 1 T.	3.0

Method of Preparation:

Mash the avocado and the lemon juice together. Add the remaining ingredients and mix well. Refrigerate covered until serving.

Makes about 1 cup.

Salsa

quantity	ingredient	carb grams
1 c.	Ketchup (p. 219)	10
1/2 c.	Pickled Onions (p. 216), diced	8
1/4 c.	pickled jalapeño peppers, diced	2
	Total Carbohydrate Grams	20
	Carbohydrate Grams per serving of 1 T.	0.7

Method of Preparation:

Mix all ingredients thoroughly.

Makes 1 3/4 cups.

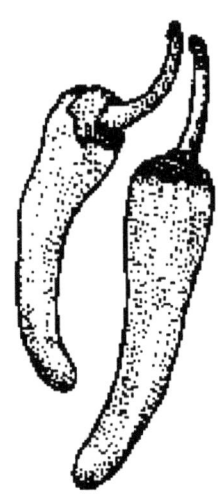

Sauce Rémoulade

It appears that Rémoulade sauce has about as many variations as chicken wings.

quantity	ingredient	carb grams
1/2 c.	mayonnaise	
1/2 c.	Dijon mustard	
1 t.	garlic powder	2
1/2 c.	Pickled Onions (p. 216)	8
2 T.	celery, diced finely	1
1 T.	Worcestershire Sauce (p. 222)	
1 T.	lemon juice	1
1 t.	sugar equivalent sweetener	
1/2 t.	salt	
1/4 t.	black pepper	
	Total Carbohydrate Grams	12
	Carbohydrate Grams per serving of 1 T.	0.4

Method of Preparation:

Mix the celery, lemon juice, sweetener and salt and let sit 15 minutes. Mix all ingredients. Refrigerate.

Makes about 2 cups.

Faux Coconut Milk

quantity	ingredient	carb grams
1/2 c.	heavy cream	3
1/2 c.	water	
2 t.	sugar equivalent sweetener	
1 t.	coconut flavoring	
	Total Carbohydrate Grams	3
	Carbohydrate Grams per serving of 1 T.	0.2

Method of Preparation:

Mix all ingredients and refrigerate until using. Stir well just before using.

Makes 1 cup.

Hint – Watch for the hidden carbs in such foods as liver and some seafood.

Index